The
Most
Amazing
Hockey
Quiz Book
Ever

The Most Amazing Hockey Quiz Book Ever

Ron Wight

KEY PORTER BOOKS

National Library of Canada Cataloguing in Publication

Wight, Ron
        The most amazing hockey quiz book ever / Ron Wight.

ISBN 1-55263-479-5

        1. Hockey--Miscellanea. 2. National Hockey League--Miscellanea. I. Title.

GV847.W493 2002   796.962'64   C2002-903448-5

The publisher gratefully acknowledges the support of the Canada Council for the Arts and the Ontario Arts Council for its publishing program.

Canadä

We acknowledge the financial support of the Government of Canada through the Book Publishing Industry Development Program (BPIDP) for our publishing activities.

Key Porter Books Limited
70 The Esplanade
Toronto, Ontario
Canada M5E 1R2

www.keyporter.com

Cover design and electronic formatting: Lightfoot Art & Design Inc.

Printed and bound in Canada

02 03 04 05 06 6 5 4 3 2 1

This book is dedicated to my Mom and Dad,
who always got me to the rink and let me stay up late to watch the game,
and to my brothers and sisters, who had to grow up
living with my hockey obsession.

Contents

Introduction

My fondest childhood memories all revolve around hockey. I remember stopping shots in the laneway and playing ball hockey with the kids down the road. I was there for every pond hockey game and always eagerly anticipated my minor-league hockey matches. I followed the exploits of my goaltending heroes, Johnny Bower and Jacques Plante, in every way possible. *Hockey Night in Canada* was the television event of the week with Bill Hewitt, Brian McFarlane, Ward Cornell and others keeping us informed of NHL events. But Saturday's telecast wasn't sufficient for my enormous hockey appetite. The best radio reception in southern Ontario originated out of Detroit. Even though I was an avid Maple Leafs fan, I would go to bed listening to Budd Lynch and Bruce Martyn broadcasting the Red Wings' games. I collected hockey cards, clipped hockey stories from the paper, and looked forward to the glossy photos of the pros in the *Toronto Star Weekly*. My dream, like so many others, was to play in the National Hockey League someday.

While I never achieved my goal, my passion for the game has only grown. I have developed a deep interest in the history of hockey, and yet continue to be amazed at the skill level of its modern superstars. Having a daughter who has played the game for the past decade, I have been introduced to the growing world of women's hockey. The outstanding skill level at the 2002 Olympics demonstrated that both the men's and women's games just continue to get better. My hope for this book is that my enthusiasm and fascination for this great game come through in the questions and answers, inspiring an appreciation of the game in others.

—Ron Wight

Setting the Records Straight

There is considerable lore and legend regarding the game of hockey. Some of it is true, while other "well-known facts" are actually myths that have been passed on through the decades and have become entrenched as hockey history. These questions will challenge your knowledge of hockey fact vs. fantasy.

First Period— Who Am I?

1. *I am the first NHL coach to perform goaltending heroics for my team.*

Odie Cleghorn, coach of the expansion Pittsburgh Pirates, made his only goaltending appearance in the NHL on February 23, 1926. Cleghorn's Pirates had lost three consecutive games and were five points out of a playoff spot when star goaltender Roy Worters fell ill with pneumonia. Without a suitable backup goalie available, Cleghorn strapped on the goal pads and stopped all but two shots directed his way by the Montreal Canadiens in a 3-2 Pirates victory. The expansion Pirates used the momentum from their coach's goaltending victory to reel off wins in six of their next seven games and squeak into the final playoff spot by one point. Odie Cleghorn's team made the playoffs in their first year in the NHL, with his goaltending appearance marking the start of their great stretch drive.

It is ironic that Odie Cleghorn, a rival coach who happened to be a spectator at the second game of the 1928 Stanley Cup finals on April 7, 1928, was then called in to replace Ranger coach Lester Patrick behind the bench when Patrick made his famous appearance as a replacement goalie for New York.

2. *I am the oldest individual to play in my first NHL game.*

Ranger coach Lester Patrick was forty-three years old when he played his first NHL game. Patrick filled in on the Ranger blueline in a 2-1 victory over the New York Americans on March 20, 1927. He had seen plenty of big-league action in the western professional leagues, but this was his first NHL appearance as a player.

The oldest lifetime minor-leaguer to finally play in the NHL was Connie Madigan. Madigan was thirty-eight years old when he hit the ice for a total of twenty-five games with the St. Louis Blues in 1973.

3. *I am the first NHL goaltender to wear a mask.*

Montreal Maroons goaltender Clint Benedict was the first netminder to wear a face mask in the NHL. Benedict wore a crude leather mask to protect a nose injury he had suffered in early January of 1930. Benedict's first game with his facial protection was February 20, 1930, when his Maroons tied the New York Americans 3-3 at Madison Square Garden. Benedict wore the mask over five games until March 4, when his nose was re-injured in a 6-2 loss to the Ottawa Senators, an injury which convinced him to retire. The masked Benedict posted a record of one win, three losses and one tie during what would be his last five games in the NHL. Almost thirty years later, on November 1, 1959, Jacques Plante would make his masked debut against the Rangers at the same Madison Square Garden.

4. *I recorded a hat trick in a single overtime period of an NHL game.*

Ken Doraty of the Toronto Maple Leafs scored three of his nine 1933–34 season goals on January 16 in Ottawa. The visiting Maple Leafs had tied the Senators 4-4 with two goals in the final six minutes of regulation time. Doraty scored at 1:35, 2:20 and 9:05 of the mandatory ten minute overtime period to record the only NHL hat trick in a single overtime period.

5. *I am the first goaltender with no big-league experience to backstop an NHL team to the Stanley Cup.*

While Ken Dryden joined the Canadiens from the minors to deliver a Conn Smythe-winning performance in the 1971 playoffs, Earl Robertson was the first Stanley Cup-winning goaltender to have spent the regular season in the minors. Robertson tended net for the Detroit Red Wings's farm club, the Pittsburgh Hornets, in the 1936–37 season before getting the call to replace injured goaltender Normie Smith in the 1937 playoffs. Robertson faced the New York Rangers in all five games of the finals, recording back-to-back shutouts in the last two. In spite of his outstanding playoff performance, Robertson was dealt to the New York Americans before the next season.

6. *I recorded the fastest six shutouts from the beginning of an NHL career.*

Goaltender Frank Brimsek recorded six shutouts very early in his NHL career, but it took him ten games, not eight as is often reported. Brimsek was in goal for the first two games of the 1938–39 season, replacing the ailing regular goaltender Tiny Thompson. During these two games, he recorded a 3-2 win over Toronto and 4-1 victory over the Red Wings. Tiny Thompson returned to tend the net for the Bruins for the next five games before being traded to the Detroit Red Wings in late November. Brimsek then took over the starting job and recorded his legendary six shutouts over his next eight starts. Brimsek topped off his outstanding start by winning the Calder and Vezina trophies, being elected to the First All-Star Team and leading the Bruins to their first Cup victory in ten years.

7. *My performance may be the most overlooked event contributing to the Toronto Maple Leafs' miracle comeback in the 1942 Stanley Cup finals.*

Toronto's 1942 comeback from a 3-0 deficit in games to win the 1942 Stanley Cup finals has taken on legendary proportions over the years. Credit for the Leafs' four straight wins has been attributed to many sources. Stories abound regarding an emotional letter from a fan that coach Hap Day read to the Maple Leafs, the benching of veterans Gordie Drillon and Bucko McDonald in favor of younger players, and a change in Toronto's offensive strategy from carrying the puck to a dump-and-chase style. However, the critical event in the series was likely Detroit coach and manager Jack Adams getting himself kicked out of the series following the fourth game. This was Toronto's first victory of the series, which still had the Red Wings leading three games to one, with an excellent chance at the Cup. Adams was suspended indefinitely by league president Frank Calder for attacking referee Mel Harwood over disputed penalty calls. Without Adams behind the Detroit bench, Toronto went on to win a couple of relatively easy 9-3 and 3-0 victories. Toronto was then able to squeak out a 3-1 victory in game seven to complete the most amazing comeback in Stanley Cup finals history.

8. *My forty-fifth goal was the most celebrated event of the 1944–45 regular season.*

Rocket Richard's forty-fifth goal in 1945 was the biggest goal in a season that would later become his legendary "fifty goals in fifty games" season. Scoring fifty goals in an NHL season has become such a landmark over the years, it is often assumed that Richard's most celebrated goal would have been his fiftieth in the 1944–45 season. However, Richard's forty-fifth goal held more significance for hockey fans at the time, as it surpassed Joe Malone's single season goal-scoring record of forty-four, which he had achieved in the initial NHL season of 1917–18. Richard recorded his forty-fifth goal against Frank McCool of the Toronto Maple Leafs on February 25, 1945, with Joe Malone being present to congratulate him as he became the NHL single season goal-scoring leader.

Paul Henderson of the Red Wings watches the puck sail past Maple Leaf Goalie Johnny Bower in a game played on October 18, 1967.

9. *I am the first player suspended for gambling on NHL games.*

Babe Pratt was expelled from the NHL in January of 1946 for his gambling activities. Pratt admitted to his actions in an appeal and was reinstated sixteen days later on a promise to abstain from betting on NHL games. Pratt's five game absence was unbelievably lenient compared to the life suspensions handed out to two players in March of 1948. Both Don Gallinger of the Boston Bruins and Billy Taylor of the New York Rangers were permanently kicked out of the league for similar gambling offences.

10. *I am the oldest individual to play goal in an NHL game.*

Moe Roberts substituted for an injured Harry Lumley of the Black Hawks in a game against Detroit in late November of 1951. Roberts would celebrate his forty-sixth birthday three weeks later on December 13. Roberts, serving as an assistant trainer, played one period of shutout hockey in relief of Lumley. Roberts had last seen NHL action with the New York Americans in the 1933–34 season. Other elderly goaltenders include Johnny Bower, Jacques Plante and Lester Patrick. Bower had just turned forty-five one month before his last NHL game on December 10, 1969, against the Montreal Canadiens. Jacques Plante played his final NHL games as a member of the Boston Bruins in the 1973 Stanley Cup playoffs when he was forty-four years old.

Plante also played at age forty-six in 1974–75, but in the WHA with the Edmonton Oilers. Lester Patrick was forty-four years old when he did his famous substitution for the injured New York Rangers goalie Lorne Chabot on April 7, 1928.

11. *I was responsible for Johnny Bower and Bert Olmstead becoming Toronto Maple Leafs.*

While Punch Imlach is entitled to his share of the glory for building the Leafs into the powerhouse they became in the 1960s, these acquisitions were not deals made by him. Leaf management, with the encouragement of then-coach Billy Reay, had begun to improve on Toronto's poor performances in the previous two seasons by claiming veterans Johnny Bower and Bert Olmstead at the June 1958 NHL meetings. Imlach first discussed the possibility of moving to the Leafs at these meetings, but didn't become a Maple Leaf employee until August of that year. Imlach's first significant acquisition as assistant general manager was Allan Stanley, acquired from the Bruins in exchange for Jim Morrison in October of 1958. Imlach fired Billy Reay in November of 1958, before the Bower and Olmstead acquisitions had begun to turn the struggling Leafs around.

12. *We were the first brothers to both play goal in the NHL.*

While Dave and Ken Dryden became the first brothers to face each other in an NHL game (on March 20, 1971), two other sets of brothers had both defended NHL goals prior to Ken joining Dave in the NHL. Odie and Sprague Cleghorn had lengthy NHL careers as players, and had both made emergency goaltending appearances between 1918–19 and 1925–26. Odie was the coach of the Pittsburgh Pirates and replaced his ill goalie, Roy Worters, for an entire game on February 23, 1926. Sprague went into the net twice, replacing a penalized Clint Benedict for three minutes in a game in 1918–19 and covering for Georges Vezina, who received a two minute penalty during a game in the 1921–22 season. The first real goaltending brothers to see NHL action were Len and Ken Broderick. Len played a single game for the Montreal Canadiens, replacing Jacques Plante on October 30, 1957. This Junior Toronto goalie was loaned to the Canadiens, backstopping them to a 6-2 victory over the Maple Leafs. His brother, Ken, who is probably better known as a member of the Canadian National and Olympic teams of the 1960s, played a total of twenty-seven NHL games in three different seasons, as a member of the Minnesota North Stars and the Boston Bruins, beginning in 1969–70.

13. *I led the NHL in goal scoring on the most occasions.*

In spite of the fact that the trophy for the leading goal scorer is named after Maurice "Rocket" Richard, Bobby Hull of the Chicago Black Hawks led the NHL in goal scoring seven of the ten seasons between 1959–60 and 1968–69. Phil Esposito is second in this category, having led the league in goal scoring in six consecutive seasons, from 1969–70 to 1974–75. Charlie Conacher, Gordie Howe and Wayne Gretzky joined Rocket Richard as the only players who led the league in goal scoring on five separate occasions.

14. *I am the first Swedish-trained player to become a regular in the NHL.*

Defenseman Thommie Bergman signed as a free agent with the Detroit Red Wings in August of 1972, and put together a solid first year in the NHL playing in seventy-five games with the Red Wings, recording twenty-one points and a plus-six on the Red Wings' blueline. Bergman's performance faded somewhat after his outstanding initial season with the Red Wings, who dealt him to Winnipeg of the WHA in December of 1974. Bergman later re-signed with the Red Wings as a free agent in 1978. He saw action in a total of 246 NHL games over six seasons with the Red Wings and appeared in four WHA seasons with the Winnipeg Jets. Bergman's initial success as a European-trained player was soon over-shadowed by Borje Salming, who signed with the Maple Leafs for the 1973–74 season.

15. *I am the last NHL goalie to play without a mask.*

It wasn't until his last six NHL games in 1973–74 that Gump Worsley finally donned a mask as he backstopped for the Minnesota North Stars. Andy Brown, of the Pittsburgh Penguins, remained maskless until his final game in the NHL on March 31, 1974, a 4-2 win over the Atlanta Flames.

16. *I have been the winning goalie in the most Stanley Cup deciding games in the NHL.*

Both Jacques Plante and Ken Dryden were members of teams that won six Stanley Cups. However, only Dryden was in goal each time the Canadiens won the Cup between 1971 and 1979. While Plante was in goal for five Cup victories from 1956 to 1960, Gerry McNeil was in the net for Montreal's Cup win in 1953.

17. *I played with the New York Rangers in 1959 and again in 1981.*

Chicago's Bobby Hull joined the New York Rangers on a post-season tour of exhibition games against the Boston Bruins in Europe in the spring of 1959. Hull returned to Europe with the Rangers in September of 1981. He attempted a comeback and participated as a Ranger in a Challenge Tournament in Sweden. This was Hull's final action with an NHL team.

18. *I am the first goalie to have recorded a goal in an NHL game.*

Ron Hextall is remembered as the first goalie to shoot the puck the length of the ice and score into the empty net in an NHL game. Hextall recorded his first goal against the Bruins on December 8, 1987, and later scored another goal in the playoffs against Washington on April 11, 1989. However, it was Billy Smith of the New York Islanders who was the first NHL goalie recognized as a goal scorer. Smith was given credit for the goal that the Colorado Rockies put in their own net on a delayed penalty call on November 28, 1979. Smith had been the last Islander to touch the puck, thereby claiming the honor.

19. *I am the only player to have three fifty-goal regular seasons with three NHL teams.*

No player has actually done this, although Pierre Larouche is often credited with this achievement. If Larouche's playoff goals in the 1983–84 season as a member of the New York Rangers are included, he is the only player to score fifty goals with three different teams in three different seasons. As a second year player, Larouche did score fifty-three goals with the 1975–76 Pittsburgh Penguins and fifty goals in 1979–80 with Montreal. However, he never again reached the fifty goal plateau in the regular season. Pavel Bure of the Rangers is probably the best bet to be the first to achieve this record. At this point in his career, Bure has bettered the fifty goal mark on five occasions, three with Vancouver and twice a as member of the Florida Panthers.

20. *I am the only individual to wear number 99 in NHL action and later become an NHL general manager.* Rick Dudley wore number 99 with the Winnipeg Jets in 1980–81. He was previously the general manager of the Ottawa Senators and the Tampa Bay Lightening, and was named general manager of the Florida Panthers in May 2002. Wayne Gretzky is a managing partner of the Phoenix Coyotes but has never been the general manager of an NHL franchise.

Second Period— Multiple Choice

1. *How many players did each team ice in the first organized hockey matches?*
a) 6   b) 7   c) 9   d) 11
c) 9. Organized hockey matches were usually played with nine players on the ice for each team until the mid 1880s. They were then replaced by the seven man game, played into the years of the game's growth to professional status. The National Hockey Association was the first to drop to a six player game, in 1911, although it did revert back to seven players for an eight game experiment in 1914. The western professional leagues were the last to drop the seventh player, known as a rover, which they did in the early 1920s.

2. *How many franchises were members in the first year of the NHL?*
a) 3   b) 4   c) 5   d) 6
c) 5. National Hockey League members included the Montreal Canadiens, the Montreal Wanderers, the Ottawa Senators, the Toronto Arenas and the Quebec Bulldogs in 1917–18.

Although still a charter member of the League, Quebec decided not to ice a team for the inaugural NHL season. The Wanderers withdrew from the schedule after four games when their arena was destroyed in a fire. Only the Canadiens, the Senators and the Arenas actually completed the 1917–18 NHL season.

3. *What was the first rival league of the NHL?*
a) PCHA b) WCHL c) WHA d) WHL
a) PCHA. The Pacific Coast Hockey Association was beginning its seventh year of operation as an elite professional league when the NHL began play in 1917–18. The Western Canada Hockey League was formed in 1921, resulting in three leagues competing for major league talent. The surviving teams of the folded PCHA joined the WCHL in 1924, known as the Western Hockey League in its final season of 1925–26. The NHL did not face major league competition for players following the demise of the WHL in 1926 until the formation of the WHA, which competed for seven seasons, from 1972–73 to 1978–79.

4. *When were the first games forfeited in the NHL?*
a) 1918 b) 1921 c) 1933 d) 1955
a) 1918. The Montreal Wanderers suspended play following the destruction of their arena by a fire in January of 1918. Forfeited wins were awarded to both the Montreal Canadiens and Toronto Arenas to balance the schedule, as these teams had only played the Wanderers once while the Ottawa Senators had faced the Wanderers on two occasions. Other forfeitures have also taken place in NHL history. The visiting Ottawa Senators were losing 5-3 to the Montreal Canadiens when they left the ice and did not return to protest a referee's call, thereby forfeiting their game, on January 26, 1921. The Montreal Maroons were awarded a 4-3 win in a forfeit in Toronto on February 27, 1926. Babe Dye, of the St. Pats, refused to give the referee the puck, leading to the official's decision.

The visiting Chicago Black Hawks forfeited a 3-2 overtime loss to the Boston Bruins on March 14, 1933. The Hawks left the ice as a result of a disputed Boston goal and didn't complete the ten minute overtime period. The last forfeiture in the NHL took place on March 17, 1955. During the game, with Detroit leading Montreal by a score of 4-1 at the end of the first period, an angry fan released a tear gas canister. What became known as the Richard riot followed in downtown Montreal.

5. *When was men's ice hockey first played as an official Olympic sport?*
a) 1920 b) 1924 c) 1928 d) 1932
b) 1924. While a hockey tournament was part of the 1920 Summer Olympics in Antwerp, Belgium, it was not recognized as an official Olympic event. The first Winter Olympics with ice hockey included as part of the events was held in Chamonix, France. The Toronto Granites, playing for Canada, won the first gold medal in men's ice hockey. Canada also took gold in the 1928 games in St. Moritz, Switzerland, with the Toronto Varsity Grads representing the country, and again at the 1932 games at Lake Placid, USA, with a victory by the Winnipegs.

6. *Which of these cities was the last to construct an artificial ice surface for hockey?*
a) Montreal   b) Ottawa
c) Toronto   d) Vancouver
a) Montreal did not have a hockey rink with artificial ice until the Forum was constructed in 1924. Frank and Lester Patrick, founders of the PCHA, had built Canada's first artificial ice surfaces in Vancouver and Victoria for the 1911–12 hockey season. Toronto's first artificial ice was for the 1913–14 season. Ottawa didn't have such a facility until 1923.

7. *When did NHL players first go on strike?*
a) 1925 b) 1957 c) 1992 d) 1994
a) 1925. A players' strike shut down the NHL for the first time in April of 1992, and the 1994–95 season was delayed and shortened by a lockout. However, the first NHL players' strike took place in March of 1925. The Hamilton Tigers, who had finished first in the NHL in 1924–25, refused to take part in their playoff series unless each player was paid an extra two hundred dollars to compensate for the fact that the NHL schedule had been increased from twenty-four to thirty games that season. NHL president, Frank Calder, suspended the Hamilton players and fined them two hundred dollars each. The Hamilton franchise was transferred to New York, where they became the Americans for the 1925–26 NHL season.

8. *Which was the first of these cities to have an NHL franchise?*
a) Chicago   b) Philadelphia
c) Pittsburgh   d) St. Louis
c) The Pittsburgh Pirates joined the NHL for the 1925–26 season. The franchise remained in Pittsburgh for five seasons before relocating to Philadelphia as the Quakers for the single season of 1930–31. Although Chicago later became known as an Original Six franchise, the Black Hawks did not join the NHL until 1926–27, a season after the Pirates had entered the league. St. Louis first had an NHL team for a single season when the Ottawa Senators relocated to the midwest city as the Eagles in 1934–35.

9. *Which NHL expansion franchises won the Stanley Cup the fastest after their entry into the league?*
a) Boston Bruins
b) Montreal Maroons
c) New York Rangers
d) Philadelphia Flyers
b) and c) Both the Montreal Maroons and the New York Rangers won the Stanley Cup in their second NHL season. The Maroons entered the league in 1924–25 and, by the end of the following season, had won both the league championship and defeated the Victoria Cougars of the WHL in the Stanley Cup finals. The New York Rangers joined the NHL for the 1926–27 season and defeated the Montreal Maroons for their first Stanley Cup in April of 1928.

Lanny McDonald of the Calgary Flames savours the 1989 Stanley Cup victory over the Montreal Canadiens.

10. *Who was the first visiting team to win the Stanley Cup at the Montreal Forum?*
a) Boston Bruins
b) Calgary Flames
c) New York Rangers
d) Toronto Maple Leafs

c) The New York Rangers. On May 25, 1989, the Calgary Flames were the first visiting team to defeat the Montreal Canadiens and win the Stanley Cup at the Forum. The New York Rangers, however, captured the Cup on Forum ice when they defeated the Montreal Maroons on April 14, 1928, thereby being the first visitors to win the Cup at the Forum.

11. *Which team had the best winning percentage in an NHL season?*
a) Boston Bruins
b) Detroit Red Wings
c) Edmonton Oilers
d) Montreal Canadiens

a) The Boston Bruins of 1929–30 had a .875 winning percentage with thirty-eight wins, five losses and one tie. However, they lost their bid for a second consecutive Cup to the Montreal Canadiens, losing two straight games in the finals. It is the lack of playoff success by this Bruins' team that diminishes its otherwise outstanding record.

12. *When were two referees first used in NHL action?*
a) 1926   b) 1933   c) 1942   d) 1999

b) 1933. The National Hockey League began appointing two referees in 1933, replacing the referee and single linesman arrangement that had been in effect since 1926. This new system, which designated a head referee and an assistant referee, remained in effect for several seasons during the 1930s until being replaced with the familiar referee and two linesmen setup. On a limited basis in 1998–99, the NHL returned to a two referee system which now included two linesmen. This two referee system has been used in all NHL games since the beginning of the 2000–01 season.

13. *When did an NHL All-Star team first play in a game?*
a) 1934 b) 1937 c) 1939 d) 1947

a) 1934. While the First Annual NHL All-Star Game was played in 1947, there were three benefit games in the 1930s which saw an NHL All-Star team iced. The first of these was the Ace Bailey Benefit Game, in which the NHL All-Stars faced off against the Toronto Maple Leafs on February 14, 1934. Two other memorial games were held in Montreal later in the decade: the Howie Morenz Memorial Game in 1937 and the Babe Siebert Memorial Game in 1939.

14. *When did the NHL players first hit the ice in Europe?*
a) 1938 b) 1955 c) 1959 d) 1972

a) 1938. The Montreal Canadiens and the Detroit Red Wings played a series of exhibition games in London, England, and Paris, France, in the spring of 1938. The NHL didn't return to Europe until the post-season of 1959, when the Boston Bruins and the New York Rangers faced each other in twenty-three exhibition games across Western Europe. The third time that NHL players skated as a team in Europe was in September of 1972, when Team Canada faced the Soviets in the Summit Series.

15. *How many individuals have been selected to a First or Second NHL All-Star Team at more than one position?*
a) 2   b) 5   c) 7   d) 8

c) 7. The NHL began naming the year-end First and Second All-Star teams for the 1930–31 NHL season. Coaching selections were included for the first sixteen years. Four individuals were named All-Stars at one playing position and later as a coach. Three other players were named to the season-ending All-Star teams at two different positions during their playing careers.

All-Star Selection	Initial Spot Selected	Other Spot Selected
Dit Clapper	Right Wing (1931, 1935)	Defense (1939, 1940, 1941, 1944)
Frank Boucher	Center (1931, 1933, 1934, 1935)	Coach (1940, 1942)
Cooney Weiland	Center (1935)	Coach (1941)
Paul Thompson	Left Wing (1936, 1938)	Coach (1940, 1942)
Johnny Gottselig	Left Wing (1939)	Coach (1946)
Neil Colville	Center (1939, 1940)	Defense (1948)
Alex Delvecchio	Center (1953)	Left Wing (1959)

16. *How many cities hosted regular season games in the twenty-five years of the Original Six era?*
a) 6   b) 7   c) 8   d) 10

d) 10. While the vast majority of NHL games were played out of the Original Six cities, four other cities hosted games during this era. The Black Hawks were having difficulty drawing crowds to the Chicago Stadium and decided to relocate a total of fourteen games between 1953 and 1956.

St. Louis hosted ten games, while Omaha saw the Black Hawks twice. Both Indianapolis and St. Paul saw a single game of NHL action in the Original Six era, 1942 to 1967.

17. *What is maximum number of head coaching appearances in the Stanley Cup finals by one individual?*
a) 12   b) 13   c) 14   d) 16

d) 16. There are not many coaching records that don't belong to Scotty Bowman but here is one that he will not reach. Dick Irvin reached the finals as a head coach a total of sixteen times between 1931 and 1955. He achieved this once with Chicago, seven times with the Toronto Maple Leafs, and on eight occasions with the Montreal Canadiens. Scotty Bowman coached in thirteen Stanley Cup finals.

18. *When did the Edmonton Oilers record their first win over an NHL team?*
a) 1977 b) 1978 c) 1979 d) 1980
a) 1977. The Edmonton Oilers were still in the WHA when they defeated the St. Louis Blues of the NHL by a score of 3-2 in an exhibition game played on October 3, 1977. Teams from the rival leagues actually faced off in a total of sixty-seven pre-season games between 1974 and 1978. WHA teams recorded a winning 33-27-7 record in these games with clubs from the supposedly stronger NHL. The Oilers' first win as a member of the NHL was over another WHA survivor, the Quebec Nordiques, in a 6-3 decision on October 19, 1979.

19. *When was the first regular season NHL game played in Phoenix?*
a) 1992 b) 1994 c) 1996 d) 1998
a) 1992. The Montreal Canadiens and Los Angeles Kings battled to a 5-5 tie in a neutral site game played in Phoenix on December 8, 1992. Phoenix hosted four more NHL games the following season, the last year that league action was held in non-member cities. The Phoenix Coyotes, the first NHL franchise representing the city, defeated the San Jose Sharks 4-1 in their first regular season home game on October 10, 1996.

20. *Which of the following pairs of teams have met the most times in the Stanley Cup finals?*
a) Toronto Maple Leafs and Montreal Canadiens
b) Montreal Canadiens and Boston Bruins
c) Detroit Red Wings and Toronto Maple Leafs
d) Detroit Red Wings and Montreal Canadiens
b) and c). As great as the Canadiens-Maple Leafs rivalry has been over the years, both of these historic franchises have actually had a different opponent for more Stanley Cup final pairings. There have been a record seven finals where the Canadiens battled the Bruins, and the Maple Leafs challenged the Red Wings. The Canadiens have faced both the Red Wings and the Maple Leafs in five Cup finals.

Third Period— Expert Trivia

1. *Is the winner of the final Stanley Cup contest always the recipient of the trophy?*

The Montreal AAA hockey club was the very first winner of the Stanley Cup in 1893. They were awarded the trophy on the basis of the best regular season record in the Amateur Hockey Association (AHA). There has been a playoff match-up in every season since 1894, but the trophy-winning team has not always played in the final game.

The Montreal AAA, who were the reigning 1894 Stanley Cup champions, defeated Queen's University on March 9, 1895, by a score of 5-1. This, however, resulted in a Montreal Victorias Stanley Cup. The Montreal Victorias were awarded the 1895 Stanley Cup because they had won the AHA league title over the Montreal AAA. On several occasions in the early 1900s the winner of the final game of a two-game-total-goals series was not the cup winner, as they had lost by a greater margin in the first game of the series.

The last time that the winner of the final Stanley Cup game has not been awarded the Cup was in 1919, when the Montreal Canadiens defeated the Seattle Metropolitans 4-3 in overtime on March 30 to tie the final series with two games each. The series was canceled due to the influenza epidemic that was sweeping North America at the time and no Stanley Cup winner was declared.

---

2. *Other than the suspended series of 1919, has there been one Stanley Cup winner per year?*

Except for 1919, there has been a single winner of the Cup every year from 1911 to the present. Prior to 1911, there were often multiple challenges to the Cup holder within the year, resulting in two different teams being declared Cup winners in the same year on seven occasions.

Year	Stanley Cup Winners
1896	Winnipeg Victorias (February), Montreal Victorias (December)
1899	Montreal Victorias (February), Montreal Shamrocks (March)
1902	Winnipeg Victorias (January), Montreal AAA (March)
1903	Montreal AAA (February), Ottawa Silver Seven (March)
1906	Ottawa Silver Seven (February), Montreal Wanderers (March, December)
1907	Kenora Thistles (January), Montreal Wanderers (March)
1910	Ottawa Senators (January), Montreal Wanderers (March)

3. *When did a player first score at a goal-a-game pace over an entire NHL season?*

It is often overlooked that the NHL had several outstanding scorers during its first season of 1917–18, who netted the puck at over a goal-a-game pace. The 1925–26 season marked the first time that no player in the league had scored this frequently. Eventually, Maurice Richard's fifty goals in fifty games became the benchmark for scoring in a single season. With Richard's achievement, 1944–45 was the only season with a goal-a-game pace between 1925–26 and 1980–81, when Wayne Gretzky recorded ninety-two goals in eighty games.

NHL Leading Scorers 1917–18		
Name	**Games Played**	**Goals**
Joe Malone,	20	44
Montreal Canadiens		
Cy Denneny,	20	36
Ottawa Senators		
Reg Noble,	20	30
Toronto Arenas		

4. *Has Toronto always competed in the NHL?*

The Toronto franchise, first nicknamed the Arenas, followed by the St. Patricks and then the Maple Leafs, has been a member of the NHL throughout the league's entire existence. The Arenas were the first NHL team to win the Stanley Cup but struggled in their second season in the league. Their record got so bad that the Arenas actually withdrew from the balance of the schedule on February 20, 1919, leaving just two active members of the league, the Montreal Canadiens and the Ottawa Senators.

With Toronto out, the two remaining clubs then agreed to proceed directly to a best-of-seven series to determine the league's representative in the Stanley Cup playoffs against the Pacific Coast Hockey Association champions. Montreal defeated Ottawa four games to one in the only best-of-seven series in the NHL prior to 1939. Montreal then faced the PCHA champs, the Seattle Metropolitans, in the only incomplete Stanley Cup final in history.

Toronto returned for the 1919–20 NHL season as the St. Patricks, and has been a continuous and active participant in every season since.

5. *When did Montreal and Quebec first face each other in NHL action?*

Hockey fans enjoyed what was known as "the Battle of Quebec," between the Montreal Canadiens and the Quebec Nordiques, from 1979, when the Nords came into the NHL as WHA survivors, until 1995, when the franchise relocated to Denver as the Colorado Avalanche. Many fans were not aware that the Canadiens had faced another Quebec franchise, the Bulldogs, in the 1919–20 NHL season. The Canadiens dominated a weak Bulldogs team, winning seven of eight games between the two clubs. Having struggled through a dismal season, the Bulldogs relocated to Hamilton as the Tigers for the 1920–21 season.

6. *What is the fewest number of playoff games ever played in an NHL season?*

There were no playoff games played following the 1919–20 regular season. Having won both halves of the split season, the Ottawa Senators were declared league champions and proceeded directly to the Stanley Cup finals against the Seattle Metropolitans, winners of the Pacific Coast Hockey Association.

7. *Why was the Montreal Forum built?*

The Montreal Forum was built at the corner of Atwater and St. Catherine streets in 1924 by a group led by William Northey and Donat Raymond. The construction of the new arena was for the NHL expansion franchise in Montreal, which came to be known as the Maroons. The Montreal Canadiens were still under contract to play their home games at the Mount Royal Arena at this time. However, it was the Canadiens, and not the Maroons, who played the first NHL game at the Montreal Forum, as the ice at the Mount Royal Arena was not ready for the season opener on Saturday, November 29, 1924. The Canadiens defeated the Toronto St. Pats 7-1 on that evening, watched by a crowd of eight thousand fans. They went on to play the remainder of their home games for the 1924–25 season at the Mount Royal Arena, while the Maroons made their home at the Forum. The Canadiens continued to play out of the Mount Royal Arena until the end of the 1925–26 season, when they were able to break their lease and move in as tenants of the Montreal Forum. The Canadiens and the Maroons shared the Forum as their home ice for the next twelve seasons, from 1926–27 to the end of the 1937–38 season, when the Maroons last played in the NHL.

8. *Which of the Original Six franchises has not missed the playoffs for three consecutive years since the 1920s?*

There has been considerable coverage of the Montreal Canadiens' absence from the playoffs in 1999, 2000 and 2001. This marked only the second time that this storied franchise had missed the NHL playoffs for three consecutive seasons. The Canadiens had previously missed the NHL playoffs for three consecutive years back in 1920, 1921 and 1922.

What has not been widely noted is that the Maple Leafs now hold this mark of regular season achievement among the Original Six. The Toronto franchise last missed the playoffs for the three consecutive years between 1926 and 1928.

9. *Which NHL city did Detroit not play in during their first NHL season?*
The Detroit franchise, initially nicknamed the Cougars, began league play for the 1926–27 season. However, Detroit had no suitable arena facility, so the Cougars played all of their home games across the border in Windsor, Ontario, during their first season. The Detroit Olympia was completed in time for their second season and remained the home of the franchise known as the Cougars, the Falcons, and finally the Red Wings for over five decades. The Red Wings moved to their present home, the Joe Louis Arena, in December of 1979.

10. *Who was the first individual to play in an NHL All-Star game, but not a single NHL regular season or playoff game in that season?*
King Clancy gets the nod, if the Howie Morenz Memorial Game is classified as an All-Star game. The game pitted the All-Stars from six NHL clubs against a squad of Canadien and Maroon All-Stars on November 5, 1937. Clancy had retired from NHL action the previous November and had moved into the coaching job of the Montreal Maroons for the 1937–38 season. While Canadiens' coach Cecil Hart coached the Montreal All-Stars, Clancy took to the ice on defense for this single game. Clancy's coaching career with the Maroons was short-lived and he found himself back on the ice as a referee later that same

season. The only other coach to play in an All-Star tilt is Doug Harvey, who skated as the player-coach of the Rangers in the Fifteenth Annual All-Star Game in 1961.

Goaltender Al Smith is the only individual to play in an annual All-Star game but not in a single NHL game that season. The Twenty-first Annual Game in 1968 featured the Toronto Maple Leafs, as defending Cup champions, against the NHL All-Stars. Al Smith had been called up as a replacement for injured Maple Leaf netminder Johnny Bower. Smith relieved Bruce Gamble in the Toronto net for the third period of the 1968 All-Star Game and stopped nine of ten shots as the Maple Leafs defeated the NHL All-Stars by a score of 4-3. This was the only NHL action Smith saw in 1967–68.

11. *Only NHL teams have competed for the Stanley Cup since 1926–1927. Since 1927, does winning your last NHL playoff game of the season guarantee the Stanley Cup?*
Prior to 1936, the NHL often used a two game total goal series in the quarter-final and, in some cases, semi-final rounds. On two occasions, a team won the final game of a two game total goal series but lost the series based on a wider goal differential from the first game. In the first instance, the Pittsburgh Pirates lost game one 4-0 to the New York Rangers on March 27, 1928. Two days later, in their final game of the playoffs, they beat the Rangers 4-2. They lost the series, however, on total goals 6-4. The last time this happened was in 1936,

when Chicago lost the first game to the New York Americans 3-0 on March 24. Two days later, Chicago defeated the Americans 5-4, but the Americans proceeded in the playoffs on a 7-5 win in the total goals series. Since 1937, there have been no two game total goal playoff series. Without these series, winning your last playoff game makes you the cup winner.

12. When did legendary Canadian broadcaster Foster Hewitt first call a hockey game from Europe?

Many will recall Foster Hewitt's play-by-play during the 1972 Summit Series. Even young hockey fans are familiar with his legendary "Henderson has scored for Canada" call in game eight. However, Hewitt had been overseas with the broadcast of an important Canadian game seventeen years earlier. The 1955 World Championships held special significance as the Soviet Union had captured their first world title from the Canadians the previous year. Foster Hewitt missed his traditional broadcast of NHL hockey to bring the country his call of Canada's win from Krefeld, Germany. Canada's Penticton Vees defeated the Soviet Union 5-0 in the final game on March 6, 1955, to bring the World Championship title back to Canada.

13. What is the connection between Bill Barilko and Toronto's 1962 Cup win?

Toronto's Bill Barilko scored his famous Cup-winning goal in overtime on April 21, 1951, to defeat the Montreal Canadiens in a hard-fought five game series. That August, Barilko and a friend disappeared while flying home from a fishing trip in Northern Ontario. Searchers were unable to find any trace of the missing fishing party at the time. It wasn't until the spring of 1962 that the crash site was discovered. Ironically, it was also in 1962, that the Leafs won their first Stanley Cup since the historic Barilko goal. Many accounts relate that Toronto's 1962 Cup followed the discovery of Barilko's remains. In actual fact, the Maple Leafs captured the Cup on April 22 of that year, while Barilko's body was not found until June 6, 1962.

14. Why was Chicago's first place finish in 1967 such a major hockey story?

Chicago's first season in 1926–27 was a very respectable showing for a new team. Under coach Pete Muldoon they achieved a third place finish in the American Division, but lost out in the first round of the playoffs. Despite doing so well, Muldoon was fired by the owner, Major Frederic McLaughlin. The Major was a very disagreeable owner to work for, firing coaches frequently even if a job was being done well. Legend has it that when Muldoon was fired, he told McLaughlin that he was putting a curse on the team so it would never finish in first place. It was then very significant when Chicago finished first in 1967, after a dry spell of so many years. In truth, though, Jim Coleman, a

Toronto sports reporter, admitted to making up the whole affair for a good story. The curse of Muldoon was just a myth.

15. When did NHL teams from four different cities play league games in the same arena on the same day?

You might think this could have happened back in 1941–42, when the re-named Brooklyn Americans and the New York Rangers shared Madison Square Garden. While MSG was the site, the two games occurred on Sunday, March 3, 1968, long after the Americans' demise. When a disastrous storm blew the roof off the Philadelphia Spectrum in March of 1968, the Flyers were forced to play their home games "on the road" while repairs were taking place. They played some of their games in Quebec City, which was home to their farm team, the Quebec Aces. The Flyers also played home games at Madison Square Garden and Maple Leaf Gardens. On the afternoon of Sunday March 3, 1968, the visiting Oakland Seals and the "home team" Flyers battled to a 1-1 draw at Madison Square Garden. Later that evening the Chicago Black Hawks were defeated 4-0 by the Rangers in their regularly scheduled game.

16. When was the NHL amateur entry draft held secretly?

It's hard to believe that the media spectacle that NHL clubs now host with such fanfare was actually an event held in private within the NHL offices in the mid 1970s. The intention of keeping the team selections under such secrecy was to out-manoeuver the rival World Hockey Association and get the jump on signing available amateur prospects.

17. When did the city of Denver first host an NHL playoff game?

Extensive playoff games have become the norm in Colorado since the arrival of the Avalanche in Denver for the 1995–96 season. However, the previous Colorado team, the Rockies, were not nearly as successful. In the six struggling seasons they spent in the Mile-High City, they only hosted a single playoff game. On April 13, 1978, the visiting Philadelphia Flyers defeated the Rockies by a score of 3-1 to sweep the best of three preliminary playoff series two games to nothing.

18. Who was the last player to have played an entire season in the Original Six era to be still skating in the NHL?

While Wayne Cashman, Serge Savard and Carol Vadnais are recognized as the final players from the Original Six years to see NHL action, none of the three had seen much league action before expansion. Vadnais had the most NHL experience of the trio, having played twelve games with the Montreal Canadiens.

The last regular from the Original Six era to play in the league was Dave Keon, who skated in seven full seasons with the Toronto Maple Leafs prior to the league doubling in size in 1967. Keon was still active in 1981–82, playing his final seventy-eight NHL games with the Hartford Whalers.

Bill Baker of the United States and Valeri Kharlamov of the Soviet Union collide during the Americans amazing 4-3 victory at the 1980 Olympics.

19. *Who did Team USA defeat in the semi-finals and finals to win gold at the 1980 Olympics?*

There were no semi-final or final hockey games at the 1980 Winter Games. The present format, with sudden death playoff matches based on placement from two pools of round robin play, was introduced at the 1992 Olympics.

The 1980 tournament involved two pools, named the Red and Blue Divisions, with six nations in each. The top two teams from each pool advanced to the medal round with the results of the game between clubs advancing from the same pool carried forward. The United States and Sweden advanced to the medal round from the Blue Division, carrying over a 2-2 tie from their opening game. The Soviet Union and Finland advanced from the Red Division, with the Soviets bringing along a 4-2 victory over the Finns to the medal round.

Medal-round play on Friday, February 22 saw Finland and Sweden battle to a 3-3 draw, while the Americans pulled off their incredible 4-3 upset of the Soviets. While not a semi-final victory, the win, combined with the Swedes' second tie, put Team USA in charge of their own destiny.

A win over Finland in their final medal round game would give the Americans the Olympic title. The final two games of the medal round on Sunday, February 24, saw the Soviet Union defeat Sweden 9-2, while the United States took the gold with a 4-2 decision over Finland.

1980 Olympics—Medal Round

Medal	Country	GP	W	L	T	GF	GA	PTS
Gold	United States	3	2	0	1	10	7	5
Silver	Soviet Union	3	2	1	0	16	8	4
Bronze	Sweden	3	0	1	2	7	14	2
	Finland	3	0	2	1	7	11	1

20. *What city hosted its first NHL game in over sixty years in 1992?*

Hamilton. The Hamilton Tigers were NHL members for five seasons from 1920 until 1925.

The final home game for the NHL Tigers was on March 7, 1925, when the Boston Bruins defeated Hamilton 2-0. The Hamilton players were moved to the first NHL franchise in New York, which began play as the Americans for the 1925–26 season.

Hamilton would have to wait over sixty-seven years before hosting another NHL regular season game. On October 20, 1992, Toronto beat Ottawa 5-3 at a neutral site game in the city that had last hosted an NHL regular season game in 1925.

Ottawa, which came back into the league in 1992, also had an extended absence from the NHL. However, this was only fifty-eight years, since they had been in the league up until 1934. Quebec City also had a fifty-nine-year gap between NHL games, leaving the league in 1920 and returning in 1979.

Leaders

Talented leaders are critical to the success of any team. By providing guidance, they challenge everyone to attain the highest standards. How much do you know about these leaders of hockey?

First Period— Captains

1. *Name the four Stanley Cup-winning captains of the Detroit Red Wings.*
Doug Young, Sid Abel, Ted Lindsay and Steve Yzerman. Doug Young captained the Red Wings to their first two Cup victories in 1936 and 1937. Sid Abel led the next three Detroit winners in 1943, 1950 and 1952, while his successor, Ted Lindsay, was captain for back-to-back Cups in 1954 and 1955. Yzerman captained the Wings to their most recent championships in 1997, 1998 and 2002.

2. *Which NHL team has had Stanley Cup-winning captains that were born in three different countries?*
The Chicago Black Hawks had captains Charlie Gardiner of the 1934 team, who was born in Scotland; Russian-born Johnny Gottselig, captain of the 1938 Cup winner; and Canadian-born Eddie Litzenberger, who captained the 1961 Black Hawks.

3. *When was the last time a Stanley Cup-winning captain did not play in the Stanley Cup-winning playoffs?*
1977 and 1979. Yvan Cournoyer did not play in the 1977 playoffs, due to injury. He had back surgery in December of 1978 and did not return for the rest of that season, thereby also missing the 1979 playoffs. In both of these years, Serge Savard was given the responsibility of the Canadiens "C" in Cournoyer's absence.

4. *Name the first captain of the Nashville Predators.*
Tom Fitzgerald signed as a free agent with Nashville in July of 1998 and served as their captain for almost four complete seasons, until being traded to the Chicago Blackhawks in March, 2002.

5. *Name the last two captains of NHL teams who led their teams to Stanley Cup victories, but were traded prior to the beginning of the next season.*

Eddie Litzenberger was captain of the Cup-winning 1961 Chicago Black Hawks, but was traded to Detroit prior to the next season. Wayne Gretzky captained the 1988 Edmonton Oilers, and was traded to Los Angeles during the off-season.

6. *What is the longest stretch of time that an NHL franchise has gone without an appointed captain?*

Six years. The Boston Bruins did not appoint a captain from 1967–68 through 1972–73. Johnny Bucyk served as captain on both sides of this six year gap.

7. *Who was the only Cup-winning captain of the Toronto Maple Leafs who has not been inducted into the Hockey Hall of Fame?*

Bob Davidson captained the 1945 Maple Leaf winners while captain Syl Apps was away on military service. The other four Maple Leaf Cup-winning captains, Hap Day (1932), Syl Apps (1942, 1947, 1948), Ted Kennedy (1949, 1951) and George Armstrong (1962, 1963, 1964, 1967) have all been elected to the Hockey Hall of Fame.

8. *Who captained an NHL Stanley Cup-winning team a record five times?*

Jean Beliveau was captain of the Canadiens for their Cup wins in 1965, 1966, 1968, 1969 and 1971.

9. *Name the four NHL captains during the 2001–02 season that were drafted fourth overall in the NHL entry draft.*

Ron Francis, Steve Yzerman, Stu Barnes and Paul Kariya.

Player	Entry Draft Selection	2001–02 Team Captain
Ron Francis	1981—Hartford	Carolina
Steve Yzerman	1983—Detroit	Detroit
Stu Barnes	1989—Winnipeg	Buffalo
Paul Kariya	1993—Anaheim	Anaheim

10. *The Montreal Canadiens traded their six captains prior to present captain Saku Koivu. How many can you name?*

Chris Chelios was traded to the Chicago Blackhawks following the 1989–90 season. Guy Carbonneau shared the captaincy with Chelios during 1989–90 and continued as captain until being traded to St. Louis following the 1993–94 season. Kirk Muller took over as captain until being traded to the New York Islanders in April of 1995. He was followed by Mike Keane, who joined Patrick Roy in a celebrated trade to Colorado in December of 1995. Pierre Turgeon was then captain until being dealt to St. Louis in October of 1996. Vincent Damphousse was the captain prior to Koivu. He was traded to San Jose in March of 1999. Saku Koivu was named captain at the beginning of the 1999–2000 season.

11. *Who was the last captain of the Winnipeg Jets?*
Kris King was captain of the Winnipeg Jets for only one season, 1995–96, the last season in which the franchise was located in Winnipeg.

12. *Name the two former Maple Leafs who were both captains during Hartford's initial three seasons in the NHL.*
Former Toronto players Rick Ley and Dave Keon both served as captains of the Hartford Whalers in their early NHL days. Ley was captain for the first season in 1979–80 and split the captaincy with Mike Rogers the following season. Dave Keon was captain for his final NHL season of 1981–82.

13. *Name the player who was the captain of both the gold medal-winning team at the first Olympic Winter Games and the first Stanley Cup championship won by the Montreal Maroons.*
Dunc Munro was Canada's captain in the first Winter Olympic Games held in Chamonix, France, in 1924. He signed with the expansion Montreal Maroons in 1924 and was the captain of their first Stanley Cup-winning team in 1926.

14. *Name the three ex-captains of the Atlanta Thrashers.*
Kelly Buchberger, Steve Staios and Ray Ferraro. Kelly Buchberger served as the Thrashers' first captain in 1999–2000 before being traded to Los Angeles late in the season. Steve Staios was the Thrashers' captain for their second season before signing as a free agent with Edmonton in the summer of 2001. Ray Ferraro captained Atlanta in their third season before being dealt to the St. Louis Blues in March of 2002.

15. *Four of the NHL's six teams named new captains for the 1961–62 season. How many can you name?*
The new captains for the 1961–62 season were Andy Bathgate with the Rangers, Jean Beliveau for the Canadiens, Don McKenney of the Bruins and Pierre Pilote with the Black Hawks.

16. *When did Wayne Gretzky and Mario Lemieux last oppose each other as captains in NHL action?*
Wayne Gretzky was captain of the St. Louis Blues and Mario Lemieux of the Pittsburgh Penguins when Pittsburgh defeated the visiting Blues 8-4 on March 26, 1996.

Wayne Gretzky captained teams in three NHL cities.

17. *Who followed Ray Bourque as captain of the Boston Bruins?*
Jason Allison was the Bruins' captain for the 2000–01 NHL season. Allison was traded to the Los Angeles Kings where he played in the 2001–02 season. The Bruins did not name a successor to Allison as captain during the 2001–02 season.

18. *Name the three individuals who served as captains of the Edmonton Oilers prior to Wayne Gretzky.*
Ron Chipperfield was the Oilers' first NHL captain in 1979–80, followed by Blair MacDonald later that season and Lee Fogolin in 1981. Fogolin served as captain through 1983, when the captaincy was passed on to Wayne Gretzky.

19. *Which NHL team had two of its former captains in its lineup in the 2001–02 season?*
Both Eric Desjardins and Rick Tocchet are former captains of the Flyers, and played with the team in the 2001–02 season. Rick Tocchet was the captain in 1991–92 and Eric Desjardins was given the captaincy during 1999–2000. Keith Primeau was the player who succeeded Desjardins as team captain.

20. *Who is the last American-born captain of an NHL Stanley Cup-winning team?*
Derian Hatcher was born in Sterling Heights, Michigan. He was the captain of the Dallas Stars when they defeated the Buffalo Sabres to win the Stanley Cup in 1999.

Second Period— What's the Link?

1. *Johnny Bucyk, Alex Delvecchio, Tim Horton, Gordie Howe, Mark Messier*
These are the only five individuals to have played in twenty-three or more NHL seasons as of the end of 2001–02. Gordie Howe leads the way, having played in twenty-six NHL seasons. He skated for the Detroit Red Wings from 1946–47 through 1970–71, and played his final season as a member of the Hartford Whalers in 1979–80. Both Alex Delvecchio and Tim Horton participated in twenty-four NHL campaigns. Delvecchio was a Red Wing from 1950–51 through 1973–74. Horton first saw NHL action as a Maple Leaf in 1949–50, and then played in twenty-three straight seasons from 1951–52 through to 1973–74 with the Leafs, Rangers, Penguins and Sabres. Johnny Bucyk and Mark Messier have also both seen action in twenty-three NHL seasons. Bucyk was with Detroit and Boston from 1955–56 through to 1977–78, and Mark Messier was a member of the Oilers, Rangers and Canucks from 1979–80 through to the end of the 2001–02 NHL season.

2. *Eddie Gerard, Dunc Munro, George Boucher, Sprague Cleghorn, Tommy Gorman, King Clancy*
These six individuals were the coaches of the Montreal Maroons during their fourteen NHL seasons from 1924 to 1938.

3. *Herb Gardiner, Bill Quackenbush, Kent Douglas, Serge Savard, Bobby Orr*
These individuals were the first defensemen to be awarded the following NHL trophies: Herb Gardiner of the Montreal Canadiens won the Hart Trophy in 1927; Bill Quackenbush was awarded the Lady Byng as a member of the Detroit Red Wings in 1949; Kent Douglas was the first defenseman to win the Calder as the Rookie of the Year, which he did as a member of the Maple Leafs in 1963; Serge

Savard was the first blueliner to take home the Conn Smythe, an honor he received as a member of the Cup-winning Canadiens in 1969; and Bobby Orr remains the only defenseman to win the Art Ross Trophy, which he first accomplished in 1970.

4. *Shayne Corson, Bryan McCabe, Mikael Renberg, Mats Sundin*
These members of the 2001–02 Maple Leafs have all served as NHL captains at some point in their careers. Sundin has been the Leafs' captain since 1997–98. Renberg captained the Tampa Bay Lightning in 1997–98. Shayne Corson wore the "C" for the St. Louis Blues in 1995–96 and the Edmonton Oilers in 1994–95. The New York Islanders' captain in 1997–98 was Bryan McCabe.

5. *Jean Beliveau, Wayne Gretzky, Mario Lemieux, Joe Sakic, Scott Stevens, Steve Yzerman*
All of these individuals were captain of the Cup-winning team and awarded the Conn Smythe Trophy in the same season.

Player	Team	Year
Jean Beliveau	Montreal Canadiens	1965
Wayne Gretzky	Edmonton Oilers	1985, 1988
Mario Lemieux	Pittsburgh Penguins	1991, 1992
Joe Sakic	Colorado Avalanche	1996
Steve Yzerman	Detroit Red Wings	1998
Scott Stevens	New Jersey Devils	2000

Jean Beliveau skates past Bob Baun in a Montreal-Toronto clash during the 1960s.

6. *Andy Bathgate, Ed Joyal, Wayne Connelly, Red Berenson, Lou Angotti, Gerry Ehman*

These were the leading scorers for the NHL's six expansion teams in 1967–68.

Player	Team	GP	G	A	PTS
Andy Bathgate	Pittsburgh	74	20	39	59
Eddie Joyal	Los Angeles	74	23	34	57
Wayne Connelly	Minnesota	74	35	21	56
Red Berenson	St. Louis	55	22	29	51
Lou Angotti	Philadelphia	70	12	37	49
Gerry Ehman	Oakland	73	19	25	44

7. *Pat Falloon, Roman Hamrlik, Paul Kariya, Rob Niedermayer, Alexei Yashin*

These were the first selections in the NHL entry draft for the five expansion teams entering the league between 1991 and 1993.

Year	Drafted	Player	Team
1991	2nd overall	Pat Falloon	San Jose
1992	1st overall	Roman Hamrlik	Tampa Bay
1992	2nd overall	Alexei Yashin	Ottawa
1993	4th overall	Paul Kariya	Anaheim
1993	5th overall	Rob Niedermayer	Florida

8. *Dan Daoust, Phil Housley, Steve Larmer, Pelle Lindbergh, Mats Naslund, Scott Stevens*

This is the NHL's rookie All-Star team from 1982–83, the first year it was selected. Lindbergh of Philadelphia was chosen goalie, Housley of Buffalo and Stevens of Washington were on defense, while Larmer of Chicago, Daoust of Toronto, and Naslund of Montreal made up the forward line.

9. *Nels Stewart, Howie Morenz, Bill Cowley, Gordie Howe, Jean Beliveau, Bobby Orr, Bobby Clarke, Guy Lafleur, Wayne Gretzky, Mark Messier, Joe Sakic*

These are the only eleven individuals to have won the Hart Trophy and the Stanley Cup in the same season. Both Orr and Lafleur accomplished this in two seasons, while Wayne Gretzky did this in three separate NHL seasons.

10. *Nels Stewart, Herb Gardiner, Roy Worters, Buddy O'Connor, Wayne Gretzky, Mark Messier*

These are the only players to have won the Hart Trophy in their initial season with a particular NHL team. Stewart, Gardiner and Gretzky all did this as first year NHL players. Accomplishing this following a trade to a new team were Worters, O'Connor, Messier and Gretzky, who achieved this honor for a second time.

Year	Player	New NHL Team
1926	Nels Stewart	Montreal Maroons
1927	Herb Gardiner	Montreal Canadiens
1929	Roy Worters	New York Americans
1948	Buddy O'Connor	New York Rangers
1980	Wayne Gretzky	Edmonton Oilers
1989	Wayne Gretzky	Los Angeles Kings
1992	Mark Messier	New York Rangers

11. *Alex Connell, Charlie Gardiner, George Hainsworth, Roy Worters, Bill Durnan*

All of these goaltenders served as captains with their NHL teams. The first four wore the "C" during seasons in the early 1930s. Bill Durnan of the Montreal Canadiens was the last goaltender to serve as team captain, which he did during the last half of the 1947–48 season. The NHL has not allowed goalies to be appointed team captains since the 1948–49 season.

12. *Brad Marsh, Phil Russell, Lanny McDonald, Doug Risebrough, Jim Peplinski, Tim Hunter*

These are the first six captains of the Flames from their arrival in Calgary in 1980 to their Stanley Cup victory in 1989.

13. *Al Arbour, Scotty Bowman, Jacques Demers, Dick Irvin, Mike Keenan, Bryan Murray, Roger Neilson, Pat Quinn, Billy Reay*

These are the only individuals to have coached in at least one thousand NHL regular season games. A class move by the Ottawa Senators put Roger Neilson behind the bench for the final two games of the 2001–02 season and allowed him to join this exclusive company. This also put Neilson in the lead as the head coach of eight different NHL franchises over his career.

Coach	Games	W	L	T	Number of Teams
Scotty Bowman	2141	1244	584	313	5
Al Arbour	1606	781	577	248	2
Dick Irvin	1449	692	527	230	3
Mike Keenan	1125	555	438	132	7
Billy Reay	1102	542	385	175	2
Pat Quinn	1072	527	408	137	4
Bryan Murray	1057	513	413	131	4
Jacques Demers	1006	409	467	130	5
Roger Neilson	1000	460	381	159	8

Regular Season Coaching Records to End of 2001–02

14. *Bob Gracie, Gerry Lowrey, Carl Voss*

These players were the scoring leaders for the final season of the three NHL franchises that left the league in the 1930s. Another connection is that all three played their first NHL games with the Toronto Maple Leafs.

Final Year of NHL Franchise	Player	GP	G	A	PTS
1930–31 Philadelphia Quakers	Gerry Lowrey	43	13	14	27
1934–35 St. Louis Eagles	Carl Voss	48	13	18	31
1937–38 Montreal Maroons	Bob Gracie	48	12	19	31

15. *Charlie Gardiner, Eddie Shore, King Clancy, Howie Morenz, Bill Cook, Aurel Joliat, Lester Patrick*

These are the members of the 1930–31 First NHL All-Star Team. This was the initial season that a year-end All-Star team was selected.

1930–31 First All-Star Team	
Goal	Charlie Gardiner, Chicago Black Hawks
Defense	Eddie Shore, Boston Bruins
Defense	King Clancy, Toronto Maple Leafs
Center	Howie Morenz, Montreal Canadiens
Right Wing	Bill Cook, New York Rangers
Left Wing	Aurel Joliat, Montreal Canadiens
Coach	Lester Patrick, New York Rangers

16. *Dit Clapper, Rocket Richard, Henri Richard, Jean Beliveau, Patrick Roy, Claude Lemieux*

These NHL players all won the Stanley Cup in three different decades.

Player	First Decade Win(s)	Second Decade Win(s)	Third Decade Win(s)
Dit Clapper	1929—Boston	1939—Boston	1941—Boston
Maurice Richard	1944, 46—Montreal	1953, 56–59—Montreal	1960—Montreal
Jean Beliveau	1956–59—Montreal	60, 65, 66, 68, 69—Montreal	1971—Montreal
Henri Richard	1956–59—Montreal	60, 65, 66, 68, 69—Montreal	71, 73—Montreal
Claude Lemieux	1986—Montreal	95—New Jersey, 96—Colorado	2000—New Jersey
Patrick Roy	1986—Montreal	93—Montreal, 96—Colorado	2001—Colorado

17. *Bobby Hull, Joe Sakic, Wayne Gretzky, Buddy O'Connor, Stan Mikita*

These individuals won both the Hart and Lady Byng trophies in the same season. Buddy O'Connor of the New York Rangers was the first to do so in 1947–48. Chicago's Bobby Hull was awarded both trophies in 1964–65, followed by teammate Stan Mikita, who accomplished this in both 1966–67 and 1967–68. Wayne Gretzky was the only first year NHL player to win both the Hart and Lady Byng, which he did in 1979–80. Colorado's Joe Sakic is the most recent player to make this list, as he was awarded both trophies for his 2000–01 season.

18. *Mike Keane, Claude Lemieux, Al Arbour, Larry Hilman, Gord Pettinger*

These individuals have played on Stanley Cup winners with three different NHL franchises.

Player	First Cup Franchise	Second Cup Franchise	Third Cup Franchise
Gord Pettinger	Rangers, 1933	Red Wings, 1936, 1937	Bruins, 1939
Al Arbour	Red Wings, 1954	Black Hawks, 1961	Maple Leafs, 1962, 1964
Larry Hilman	Red Wings, 1955	Maple Leafs, 1964, 1967	Montreal, 1969
Claude Lemieux	Canadiens, 1986	Devils, 1995, 2000	Avalanche, 1996
Mike Keane	Canadiens, 1993	Avalanche, 1996	Stars, 1999

19. *Bob Woytowich, Elmer Vasko, Claude Larose, Ted Harris*

These are the captains in the first four seasons of the Minnesota North Stars, between 1967–68 and 1970–71.

20. *John Cunniff, Ted Green, Rick Ley, Larry Pleau, Tom Webster*

These five individuals all played for the 1972–73 New England Whalers, the first playoff champions of the WHA. All of them also went on to become head coaches in the NHL. John Cunniff coached the Hartford Whalers for thirteen games in 1982–83, and the New Jersey Devils in 1989–90 and 1990–91. Ted Green was behind the bench for the Edmonton Oilers in 1991–92, 1992–93 and the first part of 1993–94. The Hartford Whalers had Rick Ley as head coach for two seasons, 1989–90 and 1990–91; he also coached the Vancouver Canucks in 1994–95 and 1995–96. Larry Pleau was the bench boss of the Hartford Whalers for all or part of five seasons, between 1980–81 and 1988–89. For eighteen games in 1986–87, Tom Webster held the position of head coach for the New York Rangers and then took the spot with the Los Angeles Kings from 1989–90 through 1991–92.

Third Period—
Coaches and Managers

1. *Name the two individuals who were head coaches of NHL franchises in the 2001–02 season and have been fifty-goal scorers in the NHL.*
Bill Barber, head coach of the Philadelphia Flyers, recorded fifty goals while playing for the Flyers in the 1975–76 season. Rick Kehoe took over as coach of the Pittsburgh Penguins during the 2001–02 season, having recorded fifty-five goals while playing for the Penguins in the 1980–81 season.

2. *Name the only two coaches to receive the Jack Adams Award as NHL coach of the year and to coach a Stanley Cup winner in the same season.*
Fred Shero achieved this with the Philadelphia Flyers in 1974 and Scotty Bowman with the Montreal Canadiens in 1977.

3. *Name the three individuals that have had the distinction of being head coach with three of the NHL's Original Six.*
Dick Irvin Sr., Pat Burns, and Mike Keenan. Dick Irvin Sr., a pioneer who coached three Original Six franchises, held the position with Chicago in 1928–29, 1930–31 and in 1955–56, his first two and his last season of NHL coaching. In between he was head coach of the Toronto Maple Leafs from early in the 1931–32 season to the end of 1939–40. He took over as head coach of the Canadiens from 1940–41 to the end of 1954–55. Pat Burns and Mike Keenan are the only other individuals to be head coach on three of the NHL's Original Six. Burns was head coach of Montreal for four seasons from 1988–89 through 1991–92. He joined the Maple Leafs for four seasons, in 1992–93 until being released near the end of the 1995–96 season. He was named head coach of the Boston Bruins from 1997–98 until early in the 2000–2001 season. Mike Keenan coached the Chicago Blackhawks for four seasons from 1988–89 to 1991–92. His next Original Six posting was in 1993–94, when he coached the Rangers to their first Stanley Cup victory in fifty-four years in his lone season there. His third Original Six placement was with the Boston Bruins when he took over for Pat Burns eight games into the 2000–2001 season.

4. *Who is the only individual to be the general manager of Stanley Cup winners with four different NHL franchises?*

Tommy Gorman was the manager of three Ottawa Senator Cup wins in 1920, 1921 and 1923. He also managed the Chicago Black Hawks in 1934 and the Cup-winning Montreal Maroons in 1935. His final two Cup wins as manager were with the Montreal Canadiens in 1944 and 1946.

5. *Name the last three individuals to take an NHL team that previously missed the playoffs into a playoff spot in their first season as player-coach.*

Red Dutton, Sid Abel and Doug Harvey all had very successful debuts as player-coaches. Red Dutton took the New York Americans, who had finished out of the playoffs for six consecutive seasons, into a playoff spot in his first year as player-coach in 1935–36. The Chicago Black Hawks, having missed the playoffs for six consecutive seasons, were coached into a playoff position by Sid Abel in his first year as a player-coach in 1952–53. Doug Harvey led a New York Ranger team that had missed the playoffs for three consecutive seasons to a fourth place position in the 1961–62 season, his first and only season as player-coach.

6. *Name the NHL teams who, during the 2001–02 season, had general managers with sweater numbers previously retired by that team.*

General Manager Bobby Clarke's sweater number 16 has been retired by the Philadelphia Flyers. Dave Taylor, of the Los Angeles Kings, is the other general manager to be honored by the retirement of his number, 18, by his NHL team.

7. *Name the only individual to have coached teams that have won the Memorial Cup, the Allan Cup and the Stanley Cup.*

Joe Primeau coached the St. Michael's Majors to a Memorial Cup championship in 1947. This trophy is awarded to the Junior Hockey Champions of Canada. He then coached the Toronto Marlboros Senior Team to the 1950 Allan Cup victory, which is for the Senior Amateur Hockey Championship in Canada. He also was behind the bench for the 1951 Cup-winning Toronto Maple Leafs.

8. *How many individuals have served the Boston Bruins as general manager during their seventy-eight seasons in the National Hockey League?*

There have only been six general managers in the history of the Boston Bruins. Art Ross was in that capacity the longest, being the Bruins' GM for their first thirty seasons through 1954. Lynn Patrick, Hap Emms, Milt Schmidt, Harry Sinden and Mike O'Connell are the five individuals who have served as GM through to the end of the 2001–02 NHL season.

9. *Name the last three Stanley Cup-winning coaches who had previously played with that NHL franchise.*

Toe Blake, Al MacNeil and Tom Johnson. Hector "Toe" Blake skated with the Canadiens from 1935–36, until suffering a career-ending injury in the 1947–48 season. Blake later coached the Montreal Canadiens to eight Stanley Cup victories between 1955 and 1968. Al MacNeil played for five NHL teams, including the 1961–62 Montreal Canadiens. MacNeil was behind the Montreal bench for their 1971 Cup win. Tom Johnson was the coach for the Cup-winning Bruins the following season. Johnson had skated with Boston during the final two seasons of his Hall of Fame career between 1963 and 1965.

10. *Name the only three general managers of the Edmonton Oilers in their twenty-three NHL seasons.*

Larry Gordon was the first GM of the Oilers in the NHL for the 1979–80 season. He was succeeded by Glen Sather, who worked in that capacity for twenty consecutive seasons until being replaced by Kevin Lowe at the beginning of the 2000–01 season.

11. *How many winners of the Jack Adams Award have been head coach of the St. Louis Blues at some time in their NHL coaching career?*

Eight. Three individuals have received the Jack Adams Award as head coach of St. Louis: Red Berenson in 1981, Brian Sutter in 1991 and Joel Quenneville in 2000. Five other individuals, Al Arbour, Scotty Bowman, Mike Keenan, Jacques Demers and Jacques Martin, are all former head coaches of the St. Louis Blues who have received the Jack Adams Award as a head coach with another NHL franchise.

12. *Name the NHL general manager who drafted Mario Lemieux.*

Ed Johnston was Pittsburgh's general manager for five seasons, from 1983 to 1988. Johnston was in charge when the Penguins made Mario Lemieux the first selection overall in the 1984 entry draft.

13. *Name the only three individuals to be head coach of the Kansas City Scouts.*

Sid Abel, Bep Guidolin and Eddie Bush. Hall of Famer Sid Abel was the GM of the Scouts during the two seasons that the franchise spent in Kansas City. Guidolin was their coach for 1974–75 and through the first forty-five games of 1975–76; Abel then took over for three games before he replaced himself with Eddie Bush behind the Kansas City bench for the remaining thirty-two games of the 1975–76 season. Bush led the Scouts to a 1-23-8 record through the remaining games. This was his only coaching victory in the NHL, although he had a lengthy career coaching junior hockey in Hamilton.

14. *Name the two general managers of the 2001–02 NHL teams from Guelph, Ontario.*

General managers George McPhee of the Washington Capitals and Doug Risebrough of the Minnesota Wild were both born and raised in Guelph, Ontario.

The Kansas City Scouts played for only two NHL seasons. Here the Scouts' Brent Hughes battles Ken Hodge of the Bruins during a surprising 3-2 Kansas City win in Boston on January 23, 1975.

15. *Name the NHL head coach who was the last player to play without a helmet in the league.*

Craig MacTavish spent eighteen years in the NHL as a forward. He was the last player to play without a helmet in the league, which he did until he retired from the St. Louis Blues in 1996–97. He is currently the head coach of the Edmonton Oilers.

16. *Name the three general managers during the 2001–02 NHL season with Hockey Hall of Fame fathers.*

David Poile, Craig Patrick and Doug Armstrong. David Poile is currently the Nashville Predator's general manager. His father, Bud Poile, played in the NHL and later served as a general manager with both the Philadelphia Flyers and the Vancouver Canucks. Bud Poile was inducted into the Hockey Hall of Fame as a builder in 1990. Craig Patrick has served as general manager of the Pittsburgh Penguins since 1989. His father, Lynn Patrick, was elected to the Hall to honor his playing career with the New York Rangers. He later worked as the general manager of the Boston Bruins for eleven seasons before becoming the first general manager of the St. Louis Blues. Doug Armstrong's father, Neil, was a widely respected NHL linesmen, who was inducted into the Hall of Fame in 1991. Doug is now managing the Dallas Stars.

17. *The Boston Bruins had nine head coaches over their first thirty-seven seasons in the National Hockey League, from 1924–25 through 1960–61. How many of these individuals have been elected to the Hockey Hall of Fame?*

Every one of the first eight individuals to serve as head coach of the Boston Bruins has been elected to the Hockey Hall of Fame. The eight individuals so honored are Art Ross, Cy Denneny, Frank Patrick, Cooney Weiland, Dit Clapper, George Boucher, Lynn Patrick and Milt Schmidt. All but Frank Patrick were elected to the Hall based on their playing careers, while Frank was elected as an honored builder of the game. The first head coach of the Boston Bruins not to go on to become a member of the Hockey Hall of Fame was Phil Watson, who took over as head coach for the 1961–62 NHL season.

18. *Name the last three individuals to serve as head coach with Hamilton in the National Hockey League. (Hint: All three were elected to the Hockey Hall of Fame based on their playing careers.)*

Art Ross coached the Hamilton Tigers to a 6-18 record as the Tigers finished in fourth and final place in the 1922–23 NHL season. The following year, head coach Percy LeSueur improved their record to 9-15-0, but the Tigers remained in the basement. Jimmy Gardiner took Hamilton from last place to first in 1924–25 with a 19-10-1 record. The Tigers withdrew from the league due to contract disputes with the players following their first place season. The Tiger players were relocated to New York, becoming the New York Americans franchise the following season.

19. *Coaches were included on the NHL annual All-Star teams from 1930–31 to 1945–46. Which one of the Original Six franchises never had a coach named to the First Team?*

The Toronto Maple Leafs never had a coach named to the NHL First All-Star Team. The only seven coaches to receive such an honor are Lester Patrick and Frank Boucher of the Rangers, Art Ross and Cooney Weiland of the Bruins, Jack Adams of the Red Wings, Paul Thompson of the Black Hawks and Dick Irvin of the Canadiens.

20. *Name the only NHL head coach to have a son playing in the league during the 2001–02 NHL season.*

Rick Wilson took over as head coach of the Dallas Stars during the 2001–02 season, while his son Landon Wilson skated with the Phoenix Coyotes. Rick Wilson saw his son's team, the Coyotes, edge out the Stars for one of the final playoff spots in the Western Conference at the close of the regular season.

GAME 3

The Guardians

Goaltenders have been considered different for as long as the game has been played. Fans have avidly followed their exploits from the goaltending pioneers, such as Whitey Merritt and Georges Vezina, to modern superstars like Dominik Hasek and Patrick Roy. While the equipment and techniques have changed drastically over the years, the basic assignment has remained the same: Keep the puck out of the net.

First Period— Who Am I?

1. *I recorded the first-ever shutout in a Stanley Cup playoff game.*
Wearing cricket pads on his legs, G.H. "Whitey" Merritt recorded the first shutout in a Stanley Cup playoff game on February 14, 1896, when his Winnipeg Victorias defeated the Montreal Victorias by a score of 2-0.

2. *I am the first goalie to record a shutout in an NHL game.*
Georges Vezina recorded the first NHL shutout as his visiting Montreal Canadiens defeated the Toronto Arenas by a score of 9-0 on February 18, 1918. Only two shutouts were recorded in the first NHL season of 1917–18. Clint Benedict recorded the other as his Senators defeated Vezina and the Canadiens 8-0 in Ottawa one week later, on February 25, 1918.

3. *I was in goal for the first Stanley Cup winners for three different cities.*

Harry "Hap" Holmes was in net for the 1914 Toronto Blueshirts, the 1917 Seattle Metropolitans and the 1925 Victoria Cougars as each of these teams won the first Cup ever for their cities. Holmes also tended goal on a fourth Stanley Cup winner, the 1918 Toronto Arenas. He participated in the Stanley Cup finals for Seattle in 1919 and 1920 and for Victoria in 1926. Holmes was inducted into the Hockey Hall of Fame in 1972.

4. *I am the first goalie to record three shutouts in a Stanley Cup final series.*

Clint Benedict was the first to achieve this in 1926 for the Montreal Maroons against the Victoria Cougars, in a best-of-five series. Only one other goalie, Toronto's Frank McCool, has ever recorded three shutouts in one Stanley Cup final series. McCool shut out Detroit in the first three games of the best-of-seven finals in 1945.

5. *I won the Vezina Trophy the first three years it was awarded.*

George Hainsworth took over the Montreal goal after Vezina's death. When the Canadiens decided to award a goaltending trophy in Vezina's honor, Hainsworth won it the first three years it was awarded, from 1927 to 1929. His 1928–29 season was especially amazing—he recorded twenty-two shutouts in the forty-four games the Canadiens played, for a 0.92 goals-against average.

6. *I was awarded both the Hart Trophy and the Vezina Trophy as a member of the New York Americans.*

Roy Worters received the Hart Trophy as the NHL's most valuable player in 1929 and the Vezina Trophy in 1931. Worters had an outstanding career with two of the league's weaker franchises, the Pittsburgh Pirates and the Americans. He was elected to the Hockey Hall of Fame in 1969.

7. *The NHL year-end First and Second All-Star teams were first selected for the 1930–31 season. I earned a position on these teams every year I was eligible.*

Charlie Gardiner was selected to the First All-Star Team for 1930–31 and again the next year, to the Second All-Star Team for 1932–33, and in his final season in the NHL, 1933–34, he was again selected to the First Team. Gardiner was also awarded the Vezina Trophy in 1932 and 1934. He played for the NHL All-Stars in the Ace Bailey Benefit Game at Maple Leaf Gardens on February 14, 1934, and also backstopped the Chicago Black Hawks to their first Stanley Cup victory with a 1-0 overtime win against the Detroit Red Wings in the fourth and deciding game of the 1934 finals. Tragically, Gardiner died as a result of a brain hemorrhage two months after his first Stanley Cup victory that June. He was elected to the Hockey Hall of Fame in 1945.

8. *I'm the only goalie to be on the ice for three overtime Stanley Cup winners.*

Gerry McNeil only played in five playoff years with the Montreal Canadiens, but on three of those occasions, he was on the ice when the Stanley Cup was decided in overtime. He was in the Montreal goal when the Leafs' Bill Barilko scored his famous overtime Cup winner on April 21, 1951. He was also in goal on April 16, 1953, when Boston's Sugar Jim Henry let in an Elmer Lach shot for a 1-0 Cup victory for the Canadiens. And McNeil was back in net the following year when Tony Leswick's shot deflected off Doug Harvey's glove and got past him to give Detroit a 2-1 win in overtime on April 16, 1954. Two other goalies have been on the ice for two Cup-winning overtime goals. Gerry Cheevers was the winning goalie when Bobby Orr scored on Glenn Hall in 1970 and the losing one when Jacques Lemaire scored on him in 1977. Eddie Belfour won the Cup when Brett Hull scored on Dominik Hasek in 1999, but lost when Jason Arnott scored on him in 2000.

9. *I am the only individual to have won both the Hart Trophy and the Vezina Trophy and yet never be selected to either the First or Second All-Star Team.*

Al Rollins saw action in nine different NHL seasons with Toronto, Chicago and the New York Rangers between 1949 and 1960. Rollins was awarded the Vezina Trophy as a member of the Maple Leafs in 1951 and won the Hart Trophy as the NHL's most valuable player in 1954 with the Black Hawks. In spite of these achievements, Rollins was never selected to the First or Second NHL All-Star teams. Detroit's Terry Sawchuk was chosen as the First Team goalie and Chuck Rayner of the New York Rangers was chosen for the Second Team in 1950–51, while Harry Lumley of Toronto and Terry Sawchuk were chosen to the First and Second All-Star teams respectively for the 1953–54 season.

10. *I played for three different teams in my three NHL game appearances.*

Lefty Wilson was Detroit's assistant trainer—and spare practice goalie—when he replaced a netminder in emergencies in three separate NHL games. He donned the pads to finish a single game for Detroit in 1953–54, Toronto in 1955–56 and Boston in 1957–58.

11. *I recorded the most shutouts for a single season during the Original Six era.*

Harry Lumley recorded thirteen shutouts as a member of the Toronto Maple Leafs during the 1953–54 season. Goalkeepers recorded twelve shutouts on four other occasions during the Original Six era. Terry Sawchuk had twelve as a member of the Detroit Red Wings in 1951–52, 1953–54 and 1954–55 and Glenn Hall did the same with the Detroit Red Wings in 1955–56.

12. *Dominik Hasek was traded following his Vezina Trophy–winning season in 2001. I was the first goalie to be dealt in the off-season after a Vezina Trophy performance.*

Terry Sawchuk won his third Vezina Trophy as a member of the Detroit Red Wings with a 1.96 goals-against-average for the 1954–55 season. He also backstopped Detroit to their third Cup in four seasons. Even with these accomplishments, General Manager Jack Adams traded Sawchuk to the Boston Bruins in a multi-player swap in June of 1955.

13. *While I have my name on the Cup once, I have the dubious distinction of being the losing goaltender on six Stanley Cup finalists with three different NHL franchises.*

Glenn Hall led the Chicago Black Hawks to the 1961 Stanley Cup championship, but he was on the losing side of the finals on six different occasions: in 1956 with the Detroit Red Wings, in 1962 and 1965 with Chicago, and in 1968, 1969 and 1970 with the St. Louis Blues.

14. *I earned the shutout the last time there was only one recorded in all of the Stanley Cup playoff games in a single season.*

Johnny Bower recorded the single shutout of the 1967 Stanley Cup playoffs in game two of the finals, a 3-0 win for the Leafs over the Canadiens at the Montreal Forum. It was the fifth and final playoff shutout of Bower's career.

15. *I had a lengthy training as a goalie in the minor leagues and played a number of seasons with the Cleveland Barons of the American Hockey League before finally getting my first taste of NHL action at thirty-three years of age.*

Les Binkley played for several minor-league teams, including five full seasons with the Cleveland Barons of the American Hockey League, where Johnny Bower had previously toiled. Binkley finally made it to the NHL and stuck as a regular for five consecutive seasons, from 1967–68 to 1971–72, with the Pittsburgh Penguins. He left the NHL in 1972–73 for the WHA, where he played four more seasons.

Dominik Hasek joined the Detroit Red Wings for the 2001-02 NHL season.

16. *I was the first goalie to be presented with the Lester B. Pearson Award as the NHL's outstanding player as selected by members of the NHL Players' Association.*

Mike Liut of the St. Louis Blues was the winner of the Lester B. Pearson Award in 1981. He was the only goaltender to receive the award from its inception in 1971 until 1997, when Dominik Hasek was selected as a Pearson Award winner.

17. *I am the only individual to be named to the NHL's First All-Star Team as a goaltender and serve as a head coach in the NHL.*

Roger Crozier was the NHL's First Team All-Star goalie for the 1964–65 season as a rookie with the Detroit Red Wings. And while Crozier saw NHL action in fourteen seasons, his head coaching career was much shorter. He was behind the bench for a single game for the Washington Capitals on November 7, 1981, in which the New York Rangers defeated Washington 3-1.

18. *I was the last member of the Boston Bruins to be awarded the Vezina Trophy. (Hint: While I was awarded my only Vezina as a member of the Boston Bruins, I began and ended my career with the Philadelphia Flyers.)*

Pete Peeters was awarded the Vezina Trophy as the NHL's outstanding goalie in 1983. He saw NHL action for more than thirteen seasons, between 1978 and 1991, with the Philadelphia Flyers, Boston Bruins and Washington Capitals. He twice led the NHL in goals-against, both in his Vezina season with the Bruins in 1982–83 and again in 1987–88 with the Caps.

19. *I was awarded the only Vezina Trophy that Dominik Hasek didn't win in the six years between 1994 and 1999.*

Jim Carey of the Washington Capitals won the Vezina Trophy in 1996. Carey was traded to Boston during the following season and never again came close to duplicating his Vezina season performance. Dominik Hasek of Buffalo was awarded the Vezina Trophy in the two previous and three subsequent seasons to Carey's single season heroics.

20. *I tended goal for Sweden in each of the last three Olympic games.*

Tommy Salo tended goal for Sweden in the Olympic Winter Games of 1994, 1998 and 2002. He was also in the Swedish goal for the 1996 World Cup and several World Championships. Salo played five seasons with the New York Islanders before joining his present NHL team, the Edmonton Oilers, in March of 1999.

A masked
Jacques Plante
follows the puck,
as teammate
Ralph Backstrom
heads behind the
Canadiens' met in
this action from
the 1959-60
season.

Second Period—
Multiple Choice

1. *It is well known that Jacques Plante was the first goalie to wear a mask in the Original Six era. Who was the next goalie to begin wearing a mask in the NHL?*
a) Don Simmons   *b) Terry Sawchuk*
c) Charlie Hodge   *d) Gerry Cheevers*

a) Don Simmons. Plante first wore his mask in NHL action on November 1, 1959. Don Simmons of the Boston Bruins was the only other NHL goalie to begin wearing a mask for games shortly after Plante. Simmons' first game behind a mask was a 4-3 loss to the Rangers in New York on Sunday, December 13, 1959.

2. *How many goalies have recorded three forty-win seasons in the NHL?*
a) 2   b) 3   c) 4   d) 5

b) 3. These three goalies have recorded three forty-win seasons:

Terry Sawchuk: 1950–51 (44), 1951–52 (44), 1954–55 (40)
Jacques Plante: 1955–56 (42), 1959–60 (40), 1961–62 (42)
Martin Brodeur: 1997–98 (43), 1999–2000 (43), 2000–01 (42)

3. *How many goaltenders have been selected to the NHL's First All-Star Team in their rookie season?*
a) 6   b) 7   c) 8   d) 9

c) 8. The following eight goaltenders have all been First Team All-Stars in their rookie season:

	Team	Rookie	Season
Frank Brimsek*†		Boston Bruins	1938–39
Bill Durnan†		Montreal Canadiens	1943–44
Terry Sawchuk*		Detroit Red Wings	1950–51
Roger Crozier*		Detroit Red Wings	1964–65
Tony Esposito*†		Chicago Black Hawks	1969–70
Tom Barrasso*†		Buffalo Sabres	1983–84
Ron Hextall†		Philadelphia Flyers	1986–87
Ed Belfour*†		Chicago Blackhawks	1990–91

*Calder Trophy winners
†Vezina Trophy winners

4. Which of the following goalies played their entire NHL career with the Montreal Canadiens and the Toronto Maple Leafs?
a) Paul Bibeault
b) George Hainsworth
c) Michel "Bunny" Larocque
d) Wayne Thomas

b) George Hainsworth played all of his 465 regular season and 52 playoff games with either the Montreal Canadiens or the Toronto Maple Leafs. In addition to playing with Montreal and Toronto, Bibeault also played for the Boston Bruins and the Chicago Black Hawks. Bunny Larocque played for the Philadelphia Flyers and the St. Louis Blues. Wayne Thomas played for the New York Rangers.

5. How many times was Terry Sawchuk awarded the Vezina Trophy?
a) 4   b) 5   c) 6   d) 7

a) 4. Sawchuk was awarded the Vezina in three of his first five full seasons with the Detroit Red Wings, in 1952, 1953 and 1955. Sawchuk's final Vezina was in 1965, when he and teammate Johnny Bower of the Toronto Maple Leafs were jointly presented the trophy.

6. How many goalies have been awarded the Vezina Trophy in three or more consecutive years?
a) 3   b) 4   c) 5   d) 6

d) 6. George Hainsworth, Bill Durnan, Jacques Plante, Ken Dryden and Michel "Bunny" Larocque, all of the Montreal Canadiens, and Dominik Hasek of the Buffalo Sabres have all been awarded the Vezina Trophy in three or more consecutive years. Hainsworth won the Vezina in the first three years it was presented, 1927 through 1929. Durnan won for four consecutive seasons from 1944 to 1947. Plante took the trophy a record five times in a row, from 1956 to 1960. Dryden was awarded the Vezina in four consecutive years from 1976 through 1979, sharing the trophy in the last three of those with teammate Michel "Bunny" Larocque. Hasek was awarded the Vezina three consecutive times from 1997 to 1999.

7. Which of the following goaltenders was never a member of a Stanley Cup-winning team?
a) Don Beaupre   b) Glenn Healy
c) Rick Wamsley   d) Ken Wregget

a) Don Beaupre was a member of the 1980–81 Minnesota North Stars, who lost in the Stanley Cup finals to the New York Islanders, but he was never a member of a Cup-winning team. Glenn Healy was a member of the 1993–94 New York Rangers, Rick Wamsley was with the 1988–89 Calgary Flames and Ken Wregget was a Pittsburgh Penguin in 1991–92 when their teams won the Cup.

8. *Which of the following goaltenders has made the most appearances in the Stanley Cup finals?*
a) Turk Broda
b) Glenn Hall
c) Jacques Plante
d) Terry Sawchuk

	Finals Appearances	Years
Jacques Plante	10	1953, 1954, 1955, 1956, 1957, 1958, 1959, 1960 (Montreal), 1969, 1970 (St. Louis)
Turk Broda	8	1938, 1939, 1940, 1942, 1947, 1948, 1949, 1951 (Toronto)
Glenn Hall	7	1956 (Detroit), 1961, 1962, 1965 (Chicago), 1968, 1969, 1970 (St. Louis)
Terry Sawchuk	7	1952, 1954, 1955, 1961, 1963, 1964 (Detroit), 1967 (Toronto)

9. *How many times have three Hall of Fame goaltenders all played in the same Stanley Cup final?*
a) 1   b) 2   c) 3   d) 4

b) 2. Johnny Bower and Terry Sawchuk of the Maple Leafs and Gump Worsley of the Montreal Canadiens, all of whom went on to be Hall of Famers, played in the 1967 Stanley Cup finals. Glenn Hall and Jacques Plante of St. Louis, along with Gerry Cheevers of Boston, duplicated this feat in the 1970 finals. They were also all inducted into the Hall of Fame.

10. *Jose Theodore was the only goalie selected in the second round of the 1994 NHL entry draft. How many goalies were selected in the first round of this draft?*
a) 0   b) 2   c) 4   d) 6

c) 4. For the first time ever, four goalies were selected in the first round of an entry draft in 1994. Jamie Storr, Eric Fichaud, Evgeni Ryabschikov and Dan Cloutier were all selected ahead of Jose Theodore, who was selected forty-fourth overall by the Montreal Canadiens. Some other goalies of note selected in this draft after Theodore include Marty Turco, Johan Hedberg, Evgeni Nabokov, Tomas Vokoun and John Grahame.

11. *How many goalies in the Hockey Hall of Fame never played a single game in the NHL?*
a) 2   b) 3   c) 4   d) 5
d) 5. Riley Hern, Bouse Hutton, Percy LeSueur and Paddy Moran all completed their playing careers before the NHL was established, and Vladislav Tretiak played for the Soviet Union.

12. *How many goalies have been named MVP of the NHL All-Star Game?*
a) 1   b) 2   c) 3   d) 5
d) 5. There are five goalies who have been named MVP of the NHL All-Star Game since the award was initiated in 1962. Bruce Gamble of the Toronto Maple Leafs was named MVP in the 1968 game, Billy Smith of the Islanders in 1978, Mike Liut of the St. Louis Blues in the 1981 game, Grant Fuhr of the Edmonton Oilers in the 1986 game and Mike Richter of the New York Rangers tended goal in the 1994 game.

13. *How many goalies have been on Stanley Cup-winning teams for two different NHL franchises?*
a) 6   b) 7   c) 8   d) 9
a) 6.

Goaltender	Cup Championships
Clint Benedict	1919–20, 1920–21, 1922–23 Ottawa Senators
	1925–26 Montreal Maroons
Lorne Chabot	1927–28 New York Rangers
	1931–32 Toronto Maple Leafs
Alex Connell	1926–27 Ottawa Senators
	1934–35 Montreal Maroons
Terry Sawchuk	1951–52, 1953–54, 1954–55 Detroit Red Wings
	1966–67 Toronto Maple Leafs
Patrick Roy	1985–86, 1992–93 Montreal Canadiens
	1995–96, 2000–01 Colorado Avalanche
Mike Vernon	1988–89 Calgary Flames
	1996–97 Detroit Red Wings

14. *What former NHL goalie has been head coach in the most NHL regular season games?*
a) Gerry Cheevers   *b) Emile Francis*
c) Ed Johnston   *d) Ron Low*
b) Emile Francis was behind the bench for 778 games with the New York Rangers and St. Louis Blues. Ed Johnston coached 596 games with Chicago and Pittsburgh. Ron Low has coached in 505 games with Edmonton and the Rangers to the end of the 2001–02 regular season. Gerry Cheevers coached in 376 games with the Boston Bruins.

15. *How many goalies have recorded a shutout and scored a goal in the same game?*
a) 0   *b) 1*   *c) 2*   *d) 3*
c) 2. Damien Rhodes of Ottawa was awarded a goal in a 6-0 win over New Jersey in 1999. Jose Theodore of Montreal scored a goal in a 3-0 win over the New York Islanders in 2001. Both games occurred on January 2.

16. *How many goaltenders played for both the New York Rangers and the New York Americans?*
a) 3   *b) 4*   *c) 5*   *d) 6*
c) 5. Lorne Chabot, Percy Jackson, Dave Kerr, Joe Miller and Chuck Rayner. Lorne Chabot played for the Rangers in 1926–27 and 1927–28 and for the Americans in 1936–37. Percy Jackson played a single game for the Americans in 1933–34 and a single game for the Rangers in 1934–35. Dave Kerr played a single game in 1931–32 for the Americans and went on to star with

the Rangers from 1934–35 to 1940–41. Joe Miller played for both the Americans and the Rangers in 1927–28. Miller had actually played twenty-eight games for the Americans in the regular season and was loaned to the New York Rangers for the last three games of the 1928 Stanley Cup finals. Chuck Rayner played for the New York/Brooklyn Americans in 1940–41 and 1941–42 and went on to star with the Rangers from 1945–46 to 1952–53.

17. *How many NHL Stanley Cup-winning teams have had a different goalie in net for the final game in two consecutive years?*
a) 3   *b) 4*   *c) 5*   *d) 6*
c) 5.

Team	Goalies
Detroit Red Wings	1936, Normie Smith
	1937, Earl Robertson
Toronto Maple Leafs	1962, Don Simmons
	1963, Johnny Bower
Montreal Canadiens	1968, Gump Worsley
	1969, Rogie Vachon
Edmonton Oilers	1984, Andy Moog
	1985, Grant Fuhr
Detroit Red Wings	1997, Mike Vernon
	1998, Chris Osgood

18. *How many goalies have recorded thirty or more wins in seven straight NHL seasons through the end of the 2001–02 season?*
a) 1   *b) 2*   *c) 3*   *d) 4*
c) 3. Both Patrick Roy and Martin Brodeur recorded their seventh straight season with thirty wins or more in 2001–02, tying a record set by Tony Esposito between 1969–70 and 1975–76.

19. *I was a goaltender selection in both the 1967 and 1970 expansion drafts.*
a) Joe Daley   b) Charlie Hodge
c) Cesare Maniago   d) Gary Smith
b) Charlie Hodge. Hodge was selected by the California Seals from the Montreal Canadiens with their first goaltender selection in 1967 expansion draft. Hodge was a member of the Seals for their first three seasons before being selected by the Vancouver Canucks in the 1970 expansion draft. Joe Daley had been claimed by the Pittsburgh Penguins from the Detroit Red Wings in the 1967 expansion draft. He also moved to a new league member in 1970 but not through the expansion draft. The Buffalo Sabres claimed Daley from Pittsburgh in the intra-league draft the day before they made their goaltending selections of Norm "Rocky" Farr and Gary Edwards in the 1970

expansion draft. Both Maniago and Smith had been selected in the 1967 expansion draft, Maniago by Minnesota from New York and Smith by the Seals from Toronto, but neither changed teams at the 1970 expansion meetings.

20. *How many NHL franchises have retired the number 1 to honor a goaltender?*
a) 3   b) 4   c) 5   d) 6
c) 5. The Chicago Blackhawks retired number 1 to honor Glenn Hall, the Detroit Red Wings to honor Terry Sawchuk, the Montreal Canadiens to honor Jacques Plante, the New York Rangers to honor Ed Giacomin, and the Philadelphia Flyers to honor Bernie Parent. While the Toronto Maple Leafs haven't retired the number, they have honored the number to respect the contributions of goaltenders Walter "Turk" Broda and Johnny Bower.

Third Period— Expert Trivia

1. *Name the only four retired goalies to play all of their more than three hundred NHL regular season games with one team.*
Turk Broda played all of his 629 regular season and 101 playoff games with Toronto, Ken Dryden of the Canadiens played 597 regular-season and 112 playoff games, Bill Durnan played 383 regular season and 45 playoff games also with Montreal, and Charlie Gardiner played 316 regular season and 21 playoff games with Chicago.

2. *Name the goalie who appeared in the most WHA games without making a single appearance in the NHL.*
Serge Aubry played in 142 regular season and three playoff games with the Quebec Nordiques and the Cincinnati Stingers between 1972 and 1977. Aubry went on to scout, but not play, in the NHL with both the Quebec Nordiques and the Los Angeles Kings.

3. *Who were the first joint winners of the Vezina Trophy?*

In 1965, Terry Sawchuk and Johnny Bower of the Leafs were declared joint winners of the Vezina Trophy. The Vezina Trophy was awarded to the goaltender(s) of the team allowing the fewest goals in the seasons from 1927 through 1981. The advent of a rule requiring teams to carry and dress two goaltenders in the mid 1960s resulted in teammates being joint winners in twelve of the seventeen seasons between 1964–65 and 1980–81. Since 1982, the Vezina has been presented to the best goalie as judged by the NHL general managers.

4. *Have there ever been more than two goalies awarded the Vezina Trophy in a given NHL season?*

Yes. In 1981, when the Vezina Trophy was still awarded to the goaltenders of the team with the best goals-against average, three Montreal goalies shared the honor: Richard Sevigny, Denis Herron and Michel "Bunny" Larocque. Larocque was traded to the Toronto Maple Leafs on March 10, 1981, becoming the only goaltender to be traded during a Vezina Trophy-winning season.

5. *Name the only goalies from opposing teams to share the Vezina Trophy in the same season, aside from the 1981 winners.*

In 1974, Bernie Parent of the Philadelphia Flyers and Tony Esposito of the Chicago Black Hawks were both awarded the Vezina Trophy when Chicago and Philadelphia tied for the best goals-against average.

6. *Name the only two NHL franchises that had three general managers who were former NHL goaltenders.*

Emile Francis served as the general manager for the Hartford Whalers from 1983–84 to 1988–89. Ed Johnson was GM from 1989–90 to 1991–92. Jim Rutherford has been the GM of the Whalers, now the Carolina Hurricanes, from 1994–95 to the present. The Pittsburgh Penguins had three consecutive general managers who were former NHL goalies. Baz Bastien took over as GM during the 1976–77 season and served in that capacity until the end of 1982–83. Ed Johnson held the GM position from 1983–84 to 1987–88 and Tony Esposito was the GM from 1988–89 into the 1989–90 season, when Craig Patrick took over management.

7. *For the five seasons between 1952–53 and 1956–57, only three individuals played goal for the New York Rangers. Can you name them? (Hint: All three are members of the Hockey Hall of Fame.)*

Lorne "Gump" Worsley played the majority of the 1952–53 season and won the Calder Trophy as the rookie of the year. He shared the goal with Chuck Rayner, who saw action in his final twenty NHL games. The following season, Johnny Bower replaced Worsley as the starting goalie and played all seventy games for the Rangers, putting

Team Canada
goaltender Martin
Brodeur.

together a respectable 2.60 goals-against average and five shutouts on a fifth-place team. However, the season after, Bower saw action in only five games and Worsley again took over as the Rangers' number one goaltender. Worsley played all the games for the Rangers in 1955–56 and all but two in 1956–57, when Bower replaced him.

8. Where did Terry Sawchuk record the first and last of his record 103 NHL shutouts?

New York. Terry Sawchuk's first NHL shutout was recorded on January 15, 1950, when he backstopped his Detroit Red Wings to a 1-0 victory over the New York Rangers. His 103rd and final shutout was achieved just over twenty years later, on February 1, 1970, when he stopped all twenty-nine Pittsburgh Penguin shots in a 6-0 victory for the Rangers.

9. Name the only four goalies to win the Vezina Trophy while playing for the New York Rangers.

Dave Kerr was playing for the New York Rangers when he won the Vezina Trophy in 1940, Ed Giacomin and Gilles Villemure shared it in 1971 and John Vanbiesbrouck won it as a Ranger in 1986.

10. Four Hall of Fame goaltenders played in portions of ten or more NHL seasons, but never won the Vezina Trophy. How many can you name?

The Vezina Trophy was first awarded in 1927, when Clint Benedict and Alex Connell were already partly through their careers. Benedict played in the NHL from 1917–18 to 1929–30 with the Ottawa Senators and Montreal Maroons. He was also a veteran of the NHA with the Ottawa Senators. Connell played in the NHL from 1924–25 through to 1934–35 with the Ottawa Senators, Detroit Falcons, New York Americans and Montreal Maroons. After a one-year retirement, he returned to play the 1936–37 season with the Montreal Maroons. Chuck Rayner saw action in ten different NHL seasons between 1940–41 and 1952–53 with the New York/Brooklyn Americans and New York Rangers. Gerry Cheevers saw action in thirteen NHL seasons between 1961–62 and 1979–80, all with the Boston Bruins except for two games in 1961–62 with the Toronto Maple Leafs. He also spent three and a half seasons in the WHA as a member of the Cleveland Crusaders.

11. Name the first three NHL goalies to be awarded the Vezina Trophy on two different NHL clubs.

Glenn Hall won the award twice as a member of the Chicago Black Hawks, in 1963 and again in 1967, when he shared it with Denis Dejordy. He shared the trophy again, with Jacques Plante, as a member of the St. Louis Blues in 1969. Plante won it as a Montreal Canadien for five consecutive years from 1956 through 1960 and again in 1962, and then shared it with Hall in 1969 as a member of the St. Louis Blues. Terry Sawchuk won the award in 1952, 1953 and 1955 as a Detroit Red Wing and then shared it in 1965 with Johnny Bower of the Toronto Maple Leafs.

12. *Martin Brodeur is one of many goalies to play in both the Olympics and the NHL. Name the first goalie to do both.*

Jack McCartan backstopped the 1960 United States team to the Olympic gold medal, then signed with the New York Rangers. He played four games in March of 1960 and another eight in the 1960–61 season with the Rangers. That was McCartan's last NHL experience, although he did see action with the Minnesota Fighting Saints of the WHA over a decade later. McCartan was closely followed by Don Head, goalie for the Canadian silver medalists in those same Olympic games of 1960. Don Head saw action in thirty-eight NHL games with the Boston Bruins during the 1961–62 season.

13. *These Canadian goaltending partners at the 1969 World Championships later faced each other in a Stanley Cup final.*

Ken Dryden and Wayne Stephenson were teammates on the Canadian National Team, and shared the goaltending at the 1969 World Championships. Dryden was in net when the Montreal Canadiens defeated Stephenson and his Philadelphia Flyers in a four game sweep of the 1976 Stanley Cup finals.

14. *Name the only NHL team to retire two sweater numbers to honor former goaltenders.*

The Chicago Blackhawks have retired numbers 1 and 35 to recognize the contributions of Glenn Hall and Tony Esposito, respectively.

15. *Name the only NHL team to have two of its goaltenders see game action in the 2002 Olympic Games.*

Two Carolina Hurricane goalies saw action in the Olympic Winter Games at Salt Lake City. Arturs Irbe played for Latvia in a 4-1 loss to Germany, while Tom Barrasso tended the net for the United States in an 8-1 victory over Belarus. Barrasso was traded to Toronto shortly after the Winter Games, where he joined Canadian Olympic goalie Curtis Joseph. Joseph lost 5-2 to Sweden in his single appearance in the Canadian net at the Olympics.

16. *The last three Detroit Red Wings to win the Calder Trophy as rookie of the year were all goaltenders. Can you name them?*

Terry Sawchuk in 1951, Glenn Hall in 1956 and Roger Crozier in 1965 were the last three Red Wings to be named rookie of the year.

17. *Name the first goaltender to not participate in any playoff games in his Vezina Trophy-winning season.*

Charlie Hodge shared the 1966 Vezina Trophy with Lorne "Gump" Worsley. Gump Worsley played all ten playoff games for the Cup-winning Canadiens that season. However, Charlie Hodge did not tend goal in any of these playoff games, marking the first time the Vezina Trophy winner did not play in the playoffs

18. *Name the first five goalies to have been a top five selection in the NHL amateur/entry draft.*

Ray Martiniuk, John Davidson, Tom Barrasso, Roberto Luongo and Rick DiPietro were the first five goalies to have been selected in the top five overall. The Montreal Canadiens chose Ray Martiniuk fifth overall in the 1970 amateur draft. John Davidson was chosen fifth overall in 1973 by the St. Louis Blues, Tom Barrasso was chosen fifth overall in 1983 by the Buffalo Sabres and Roberto Luongo was chosen fourth overall by the New York Islanders in 1997. Rick DiPietro was the first goalie ever chosen first overall, as a selection of the New York Islanders in the 2000 draft.

19. *Name the only three goalies to play in the five All-Star games between 1956 and 1960.*

Jacques Plante tended goal for the Montreal Canadiens for all five of these games, while Glenn Hall and Terry Sawchuk were the only two goaltenders to see action for the NHL All-Stars. The two split the 1956 game, while Hall was the lone goalie in 1957, 1958 and 1960 and Sawchuk played the entire game in 1959.

20. *Name the winning goalies in the gold medal games of the last four Olympics.*

Mikhail Shtalenkov was in goal as the Unified Team, representing the former Soviet Union, defeated Canada 3-1 to win the gold medal at the 1992 Olympic Games in Albertville, France. Sweden defeated Canada 3-2 in a shootout with Tommy Salo in the net for the final game at Lillehammer, Norway, in 1994. Dominik Hasek included a 1-0 gold medal win over Russia in his heroics in Nagano, Japan, in 1998, while Martin Brodeur was solid in the Canadian net for a 5-2 gold medal victory over the United States in the 2002 Olympic Winter Games at Salt Lake City.

Notable Names

Many athletes have gained fame through their outstanding achievements in the game of hockey and raising the bar of superior performance. Determine your level of trivia excellence by trying to identify these notable names.

First Period— Famous Firsts

1. *Name the first player to win the Olympic gold medal and the Stanley Cup in the same NHL season.*
Ken Morrow was a member of the USA Miracle on Ice at the 1980 Olympics. He then joined the New York Islanders, who won their first Stanley Cup later that same year.

2. *Name the first European-trained player to win the Norris Trophy.*
Nicklas Lidstrom of the Detroit Red Wings first won the Norris Trophy in 2000–01. He was the first player trained in Europe to do so.

3. *Who scored the first NHL goal in the Montreal Forum?*
Billy Boucher of the Montreal Canadiens scored the first goal in a 7-1 win over the Toronto St. Patricks on November 29, 1924.

4. *Name the first Finnish player elected to the Hockey Hall of Fame.*
Jari Kurri was inducted into the Hockey Hall of Fame in 2001. Kurri recorded 1398 points in 1251 regular season games with five teams over seventeen NHL seasons. He recorded another 233 points in 200 playoff games and won five Stanley Cups as a member of the Edmonton Oilers.

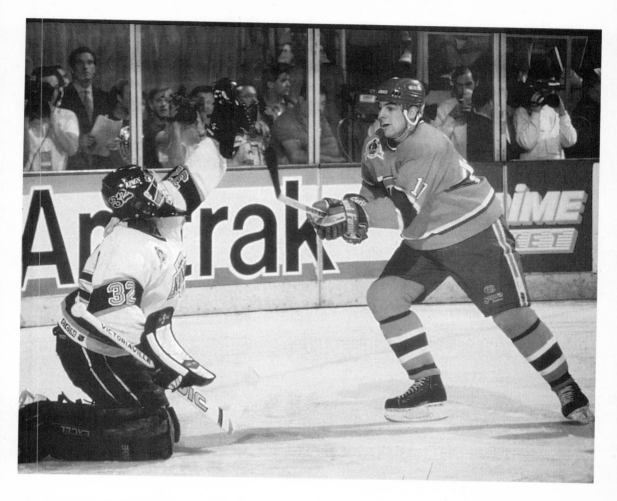

5. *Name the first NHL player to record two consecutive overtime winners in the Stanley Cup finals.*

Don Raleigh of the New York Rangers recorded overtime winners in games four and five of the Stanley Cup finals in 1950. Raleigh scored at 8:34 of overtime to give the Rangers a 4-3 victory and tie the series at two games each with Detroit on April 18, 1950. Two nights later, Raleigh potted another winner 1:38 into overtime for a 2-1 Ranger win. The Red Wings went on to defeat the Rangers in games six and seven and capture the Cup in spite of Raleigh's heroics.

6. *Who was the first player to record eight points in an NHL playoff game?*

Patrik Sundstrom of the New Jersey Devils scored three goals and added five assists in a 10-4 victory over the Washington Capitals in game three of the 1988 division finals. Mario Lemieux is the only other player to duplicate this feat to date. Lemieux recorded five goals and three assists in a 10-7 Pittsburgh victory over Philadelphia in game five of the 1989 division finals.

Montreal's John LeClair faces Kings' netminder Kelly Hrudey in game four of the 1993 Stanley Cup finals. LeClair scored the overtime winner in both games three and four of the series.

7. *Who scored the first goal in the National Hockey League for the Los Angeles Kings?*
Brian Kilrea scored the first and fourth goals for the Kings in a 4-2 win over the visiting Philadelphia Flyers on October 14, 1967. While Kilrea only scored one other goal in his twenty-six game career in the NHL, he went on to become a very successful coach in Canadian junior hockey with the Ottawa 67's.

8. *Name the first player to win the Conn Smythe Trophy twice.*
Bobby Orr is the first of only five individuals to have won the Conn Smythe Trophy more than once. He remains the only defenseman to have won the trophy on two occasions, which he did in 1970 and 1972.

9. *Who was the first Soviet player drafted by an NHL team?*
Viktor Khatulev was chosen 160th overall in the 1975 NHL amateur draft by the Philadelphia Flyers. Khatulev, who played center for Dynamo Riga when drafted, never played in the NHL.

10. *Who scored the first overtime Stanley Cup winner in hockey history?*
Hockey Hall of Famer Dan Bain scored four minutes into overtime on January 31, 1901, to give his Winnipeg Victorias a 2-1 victory over the Montreal Shamrocks.

11. *Name the only NHL player to be the captain of Stanley Cup winners with two different franchises.*
Mark Messier was the Cup-winning captain of the 1990 Edmonton Oilers and the 1994 New York Rangers.

12. *Who was the first player to receive both the Art Ross and Maurice "Rocket" Richard trophies?*
Jarome Iginla of the Calgary Flames received both the Art Ross Trophy as the leading point-getter and the Maurice "Rocket" Richard Trophy as the leading goal-scorer for the 2001–02 season.

13. *Name the first NHL player in history to have the initials "ZZ."*
Zarley Zalapski played defense for Pittsburgh, Hartford, Calgary, Montreal and Philadelphia in twelve different seasons from 1987–88 through 1999–2000.

14. *Name the first player to win the MVP in an NHL All-Star game while not representing an Original Six franchise.*
Greg Polis of the Pittsburgh Penguins was named MVP of the 1973 All-Star Game, which was played at Madison Square Garden. Polis scored two goals for the West Division All-Stars in a losing effort as the East won 5-4 in the twenty-sixth annual game.

15. *Name the only individual to play for the first Stanley Cup-winning team of one NHL franchise and be the head coach of the first Stanley Cup-winning team of another franchise since 1967.*
Terry Crisp played for the 1974 Philadelphia Flyers and was head coach of the 1989 Calgary Flames.

16. *Name the first player to have won both the Hart and Selke trophies in the same season.*
Sergei Fedorov is the only player to achieve this feat to date. Fedorov won both the Hart Trophy as the league's most valuable player and the Selke Trophy as the league's best defensive forward in 1993–94.

17. *Who was the first player to both record fifty goals and win the Stanley Cup in the same season?*
Phil Esposito was the first to do this in 1972. Eight fifty-goal seasons had been recorded prior to 1971–72, but none of the five players reaching this milestone had also been on a Cup winner in the same season until 1971–72.

18. *Name the only player to win a Stanley Cup as a member of both the New York Islanders and the Edmonton Oilers.*
Billy Carroll was a member of three Cup-winning Islanders teams from 1981 through 1983, and was then a member of the 1985 Stanley Cup-winning Edmonton Oilers.

19. *Name the player booed by his hometown fans when he won the Art Ross Trophy as the leading scorer in the NHL.*
Bernie Geoffrion of the Montreal Canadiens was the league leader in points for the 1954–55 season. Unfortunately for Geoffrion, it was his suspended teammate and fan favorite Maurice Richard that he surpassed in league scoring during the final weekend of the regular season. Emotions remained so high regarding Richard's season-ending punishment that Geoffrion was booed when he was presented with the Art Ross Trophy in 1955.

20. *Name the forward who was a member of the first Cup-winning teams in both New York and Chicago.*
Paul Thompson was a member of the 1927–28 New York Rangers, as well as the 1933–34 Chicago Black Hawks. Thompson won a third Cup with Chicago in 1938.

Second Period— Dynamic Duos

1. *Name the last two players to score over seventy goals in a single NHL season.*
Both Alexander Mogilny of the Buffalo Sabres and Teemu Selanne of the Winnipeg Jets recorded seventy-six goals in the 1992–93 season.

2. *Name the only two goaltenders in the Hockey Hall of Fame who played with both the Toronto Maple Leafs and the Montreal Canadiens during their careers.*
George Hainsworth and Jacques Plante. Hainsworth entered the league with the Montreal Canadiens winning three straight Vezina trophies and backstopping the Canadiens to Cup victories in 1930 and 1931. After seven solid seasons in the Canadiens net, he was dealt to Toronto in 1933, where he played for the next three seasons. His final season in the league, 1936–37, saw him play three games with the Maple Leafs and the final four with the Canadiens, who re-signed Hainsworth as a free agent in November of 1936.

Plante made his first appearance in the Montreal net during the 1952–53 season, becoming a regular by 1954–55 and putting together an outstanding string of five consecutive Vezina trophies during the Canadiens' five consecutive Cups between 1956 and 1960. Plante was also awarded the Hart as league MVP in 1961–62, but was traded to the New York Rangers a season later. Following a retirement and a successful return to the league with the St. Louis Blues, Plante joined the Leafs playing in the 1970–71 season and spent the better part of three seasons with the Leafs until being dealt to the Bruins in March of 1973.

3. *Name the two Finnish players who were both drafted third overall by the Los Angeles Kings in the NHL entry draft.*
Aki Berg was selected third overall in the 1995 entry draft, while Olli Jokinen was selected third overall by the LA Kings in 1997. Berg and Jokinen are the second highest selections ever of Finnish players in the NHL entry draft. LA, however, hasn't held on to these high draft picks. Aki Berg was with the Toronto Maple Leafs, while Olli Jokinen was with the Florida Panthers at the close of the 2001–02 NHL season.

4. *Name the only coach and player to team up for consecutive Stanley Cups with two different franchises.*
Coach Tommy Gorman and defenseman Lionel Conacher were together on consecutive Cup winners with the 1934 Chicago Black Hawks and the 1935 Montreal Maroons.

5. *Name the last two NHL players to score the Stanley Cup-winning goal in their final NHL game.*
Bill Barilko and Jacques Lemaire. Bill Barilko scored the dramatic overtime winning goal to lead the Toronto Maple Leafs to the 1951 Stanley Cup. Tragically, Barilko was killed in a plane crash later that summer. Jacques Lemaire scored the winning goal for the Montreal Canadiens as they defeated the New York Rangers in the 1979 Stanley Cup final. Lemaire retired following the season.

6. *Name the two NHL regulars who missed the Stanley Cup playoffs for eight consecutive seasons in the 1960s.*
Johnny Bucyk and Murray Oliver. Bucyk was a member of the Bruins in the eight straight years that they missed the playoffs from 1960 to 1967. Murray Oliver was a teammate of Bucyk's for seven of those seasons, missing the playoffs with the Bruins from 1961 through 1967. Oliver was traded to and missed the playoffs as a member of the Toronto Maple Leafs in 1968.

7. *Who are the only two players to win the Lady Byng Trophy in both their second and third seasons in the NHL?*
Dave Keon of the Toronto Maple Leafs followed up his Calder Trophy season in 1960–61 by receiving the Lady Byng in 1962 and 1963. Paul Kariya picked up the Lady Byng Trophy for his play in 1995–96 and 1996–97.

8. *Name the only two individuals to have won six different individual NHL trophies.*
Bobby Orr and Mario Lemieux.

Bobby Orr
Calder Trophy, 1967; Norris Trophy, 1968 to 1975; Conn Smythe Trophy, 1970, 1972; Art Ross Trophy, 1970, 1975; Hart Trophy, 1970, 1971, 1972; Pearson Award, 1975.

Mario Lemieux
Calder Trophy, 1985; Art Ross Trophy, 1988, 1989, 1992, 1993, 1996, 1997; Hart Trophy, 1988, 1993, 1996; Pearson Award, 1986, 1988, 1993, 1996; Conn Smythe Trophy, 1991, 1992; Masterton Trophy, 1993.

---

9. *Name the two defensemen who had not made an NHL appearance in over a decade when they took to the ice with the Flyers in the late 1960s.*
Expansion opened up new opportunities for veteran minor-league players. Dick Cherry, brother of Don, had last played in the NHL in 1956–57 as a member of the Boston Bruins when he took to the ice with the Flyers in 1968. Larry Zeidel had last seen NHL action as a member of the Chicago Black Hawks in 1953–54 before getting back to the league as a member of the Flyers' defense in 1967.

10. *Name the only two goalies to play for both the Montreal Maroons and the Montreal Canadiens.*
Lorne Chabot and Abbie Cox. Lorne Chabot tended the net for a single season with both the Canadiens in 1933–34 and the Maroons in 1935–36 near the end of his eleven-year NHL career. Abbie Cox played one game for the Montreal Maroons in the 1929–30 season and one for the Canadiens in 1935–36. His entire NHL career spanned five games. Other than the two in Montreal, he played two with the Detroit Red Wings and one with the New York Americans, in 1933–34.

11. *Name the only two players to score a Stanley Cup overtime winner in game seven.*
Pete Babando and Tony Leswick are the only two individuals to have scored the Stanley Cup-winning goal in overtime in a seventh and deciding game. In the 1950 final, Pete Babando scored at 28:31 of overtime to give the Detroit Red Wings a 4-3 win over the New York Rangers in the seventh game. In 1954, Tony Leswick of Detroit scored at 4:20 of overtime to give the Red Wings a 2-1 win over the Montreal Canadiens in the seventh game of the Stanley Cup finals.

12. *These two defensemen had outstanding rookie seasons with their respective teams during the 2001–02 NHL season. Both were first round selections in the NHL entry draft and wore the number 44 for their respective NHL clubs.*
Both Nick Boynton of the Boston Bruins and Rostislav Klesla of the Colombus Blue Jackets averaged over eighteen minutes per game with their teams during the 2001–02 NHL season. Boynton had been selected twenty-first overall in the 1999 entry draft by the Bruins and recorded eighteen points and an impressive plus-eighteen, while being a regular on a Bruins team that soared to first place in the Eastern Conference in 2002. Klesla was Colombus' first-ever selection in an entry draft, being chosen fifth overall in 2000. He recorded an impressive eight goals and eight assists and a minus-six rating in the second season of the Colombus Blue Jackets.

13. *These Hall of Famers both wore the same sweater number, won the same trophy, and were on six Stanley Cup winners in their separate careers with the Montreal Canadiens.*
Doug Harvey and Jacques Laperriere both wore number 2 while playing defense for the Montreal Canadiens. The number has since been retired in Harvey's honor. Harvey won six Norris trophies and nine First All-Star Team selections as a member of the Canadiens, where he played from 1947–48 through 1960–61. Harvey was also a member of six Cup winners with the Canadiens during these years. Laperriere won the Calder Trophy as rookie of the year in 1963–64 and followed up with selections to the NHL's First All-Star Team in the following two seasons, being awarded the Norris as the NHL's outstanding defenseman in 1966. Laperriere was a member of six Cup-winning Montreal teams during his career with the Canadiens prior to his retirement in 1974.

14. *Name the two former Red Wing teammates that made five appearances with NHL teams in the Stanley Cup finals, and yet were never on a Stanley Cup-winning team.*

Bruce MacGregor and Norm Ullman. MacGregor and Ullman were teammates on four Red Wings teams that were Stanley Cup finalists in 1961, 1963, 1964 and 1966. Ullman was also a member of the Red Wings when they were finalists in 1956. MacGregor was a member of the 1972 finalist New York Rangers.

15. *Maurice Richard went from fourth to second place in career NHL goals during the 1950–51 season. Name the two players he passed in career goals in January of 1951.*

Richard scored his 271st goal of his NHL career on January 6, 1951, as the Canadiens defeated the visiting Red Wings 5-2. This goal put him one ahead of Aurel Joliat and tied him in career scoring with Howie Morenz. Richard recorded a hat trick in a 3-0 defeat of the Rangers in the Canadiens' next game four nights later in New York to put him second in career goals. Richard would become the leader in NHL goals scored a year and a half later in November of 1952, netting his 325th career goal, which put him ahead of Nels Stewart.

16. *Name the two players who skated with the 1960 Canadian Olympic team and went on to become Calder Trophy winners.*

Dave Keon of St. Michael's Majors had a one game tryout with Canada's 1960 Olympic representatives, the Kitchener-Waterloo Dutchmen, a month before the Squaw Valley Games. The Dutchmen wanted Keon to join them immediately, but St. Mike's was only agreeable to a short-term loan of Keon closer to the Olympics. The Olympic team decided to add Bobby Rousseau of the Brockville Canadians, who was permitted to join the team for their entire schedule through the upcoming Winter Games. The Dutchmen, with Rousseau in their lineup, were silver medalists in 1960.

Keon was the Calder Trophy winner as a member of the Maple Leafs the next season. Rousseau followed Keon as the NHL rookie of the year for the 1961–62 season.

17. *Name the two defensemen who scored the most goals in the 2001–02 season while wearing the sweater number 55.*

Sergei Gonchar, of the Washington Capitals, and Vancouver Canuck Ed Jovanoski both wear the sweater number 55. In the 2001–02 season, Gonchar led all defensemen with twenty-six goals, while Jovanoski netted seventeen.

Maurice "Rocket" Richards attempts to elude Bob Dill of the Rangers in NHL play during the mid-1940s

18. *Who are the only two NHL presidents to have skated in NHL action?*

Red Dutton, the second president in league history, was an NHL player with the Montreal Maroons and the New York Americans from 1926–27 through to 1935–36. Dutton then became the coach and manager of the Americans until their demise in 1942. In 1943, he became interim league president for three years following the death of Frank Calder. Dutton's replacement, lawyer Clarence Campbell, who served as NHL president from 1946 to 1977, had been an NHL referee in the 1930s.

19. *Name the only two players who entered the 2002 playoffs with the same teams for whom they had previously scored Stanley Cup-winning goals.*

Darren McCarty scored a Cup-winning goal for the Red Wings in 1997 and Alex Tanguay netted the Cup winner for the Colorado Avalanche in 2001. These are the only two players who entered the 2002 playoffs with the same teams for whom they had already scored Cup winners.

Mark Messier scored the Cup-winning goal for the New York Rangers in 1994. He played three years in Vancouver, returned, and was again a member of the Rangers at the end of the 2001–02 season. However, the Rangers did not qualify for the 2002 playoffs.

20. *Name the two players that were new captains for the entire 1956–57 NHL season.*

Red Kelly of the Detroit Red Wings and Maurice "Rocket" Richard of the Montreal Canadiens were both named captains of their teams for the 1956–57 season.

Third Period— Three Stars

1. *Name the three 2001 NHL trophy winners who started the 2001–02 NHL season with a new team.*

Player	2001 Team	2001 Award	New NHL Team
Jaromir Jagr	Pittsburgh Penguins	Art Ross Trophy	Washington Capitals
Dominik Hasek	Buffalo Sabres	Vezina Trophy	Detroit Red Wings
Adam Graves	New York Rangers	Bill Masterton Trophy	San Jose Sharks

2. *When was the first time that three members of the same team finished in the top three in the NHL scoring race?*

The first time was in 1939–40, when all three members of Boston's Kraut Line—Milt Schmidt, Woody Dumart and Bobby Bauer—finished in the top three in the scoring race.

3. *Name the first three players to record one hundred points in a single NHL season.*

Phil Esposito, Bobby Hull and Gordie Howe all achieved this feat for the first time in the 1968–69 season.

NHL Scoring Leaders, 1968–69				
Player	GP	G	A	PTS
Phil Esposito, Boston	74	49	77	126
Bobby Hull, Chicago	76	58	49	107
Gordie Howe, Detroit	76	44	59	103

4. *Name the three players who shared a team leading eighteen goals as members of the first-year Minnesota Wild in 2000–01.*

Marian Gaborik, Wes Walz and Darby Hendrickson all tied for the team lead with eighteen goals with the Minnesota Wild in 2000–01.

5. *Who were the three non-Canadians to represent the NHL in the 1979 Challenge Cup versus the Soviet national team?*

Borje Salming, Anders Hedberg and Ulf Nilsson of Sweden were the only non-Canadians to participate on Team NHL in the 1979 Challenge Cup.

6. *Name the three highest career point leaders who have never won an Art Ross Trophy.*

Player	GP	G	A	PTS
Mark Messier	1602	658	1146	1804
Ron Francis	1569	514	1187	1701
Steve Yzerman	1362	658	1004	1662

7. *Name the three Montreal skaters who were the only players to be named centers for the NHL's First All-Star Team in the eight seasons, from 1953–54 to 1960–61.*

Jean Beliveau was the NHL's First All-Star team center for six of these seasons, with teammates Kenny Mosdell being named First Team center in 1953–54 and Henri Richard receiving the honor in 1957–58.

8. *Name the three Los Angeles Kings who made up the "Crown" Line.*

Marcel Dionne centered left-winger Charlie Simmer and right-winger Dave Taylor to make up this dominant line of the late 1970s and early 1980s. Their best season as a line was 1980–81, when they each recorded over one hundred points and finished in the top ten in league scoring.

9. *Name the three future Hall of Famers who played defense for the Toronto Maple Leafs in 1968–69.*

Tim Horton, Pierre Pilote and Marcel Pronovost. Horton spent the majority of his Hall of Fame career on the Toronto blue line, while Marcel Pronovost played in his final five NHL seasons with the Leafs. Pierre Pilote followed his outstanding career on Chicago's defense with a final season with the Maple Leafs in 1968–69.

10. *Name the three players who represented the NHL All-Stars in the 1939 Babe Siebert Memorial Game and were on the ice again for the First Annual NHL All-Star Game in 1947.*
Syl Apps, Bobby Bauer and Frank Brimsek all skated for the All-Stars in 1939. Apps was a member of the Leafs, while Brimsek and Bauer represented the Bruins on the All-Stars during the 1947 classic.

11. *Name the only three players to lead the NHL in points in the same season that their team finished last overall in the league.*
Joe Malone of the 1919–20 Quebec Bulldogs, Sweeney Schriner of the 1936–37 New York Americans and Max Bentley of the 1946–47 Chicago Black Hawks are the only three individuals to have led the league in scoring while being a member of a last place team in the league.

12. *Name the only three players to finish in the top ten in league scoring after being involved in the same trade during the NHL season.*
Gaye Stewart and Bud Poile finished fourth and sixth in league scoring respectively after being two of five players moved from Toronto to Chicago in the 1947–48 season. Max Bentley came to Toronto in the same trade, and finished fifth in league scoring.

13. *Name the first three players to win the Hart Trophy while scoring fifty goals in that same season.*
Bernie Geoffrion was the first to do this in 1960–61, followed by Bobby Hull in 1965–66 and Phil Esposito in 1973–74. Many of the first individuals to record fifty goals in a single NHL season were not rewarded with the Hart Trophy. Elmer Lach was presented the Hart in 1944–45 when Rocket Richard recorded fifty goals. Bobby Hull and Phil Esposito won the Hart Trophy in only one of their five fifty-goal NHL seasons.

Captain Bobby Clarke of the NHL All-Stars is pursued by Helmut Balderis of the Soviet Union, while Denis Potvin looks on during the 1979 Challenge Cup.

14. *Name the three players who were traded in the off-season following their Conn Smythe Trophy performance for the Cup winners.*
Wayne Gretzky, Claude Lemieux and Mike Vernon were winners of the Conn Smythe Trophy who were traded prior to the beginning of the next NHL season. Gretzky won the Conn Smythe in 1988 with the Edmonton Oilers and was traded to Los Angeles in August of that year. Claude Lemieux won the Conn Smythe Trophy as a member of the New Jersey Devils in 1995 and was ended up in Colorado via the New York Islanders in October of 1995. Mike Vernon was awarded the Smythe with the 1997 Detroit Red Wings before being dispatched to San Jose in August of 1997.

15. *Name the first three players to win the Hart Trophy but not participate in the NHL playoffs that season.*
The first to do this was Billy Burch of the Hamilton Tigers. Burch was the recipient of the Hart Trophy in 1925, but his first place Tigers didn't compete in the playoffs due to a walkout regarding a monetary dispute. Tom Anderson won the Hart Trophy as a member of the last place Brooklyn Americans in 1942, while goaltender Al Rollins won it as a member of the last place Chicago Black Hawks in 1954.

16. *Name the top three players in points-per-game during the 2001–02 NHL season.*

Player	Points	GP	Points per Game
Mario Lemieux, Pittsburgh	31	24	1.29
Todd Bertuzzi, Vancouver	85	72	1.18
Jarome Iginla, Calgary	96	82	1.17

17. *Name the three players who played for both the Colorado Avalanche in 2001–02 and Team Canada 2002.*
Adam Foote, Rob Blake and Joe Sakic were all members of the Avalanche in the 2001–02 season. They were also all members of the gold medal-winning Canadian Olympic team.

18. *Name the MVPs of the first three Canada Cup tournaments.*
Bobby Orr was selected MVP of the first Canada Cup Tournament in 1976, in spite of playing on his failing knees. Vladislav Tretiak was chosen in 1981 as he backstopped the Soviets to their only Canada Cup title. Forward John Tonelli was named MVP in 1984, as his performance was instrumental in Canada winning its second tournament title.

19. *Name the three NHL trophy winners with the Atlanta Flames.*
Two members of the team were selected rookie of the year. Eric Vail was awarded the Calder Trophy in 1975 and Willi Plett followed in 1977. The only other Atlanta Flame to be presented with NHL hardware was Bob MacMillan, who won the Lady Byng in 1979.

20. *Name the three players who were teammates on Cup winners with three different teams.*
Frank Foyston, Happy Holmes and Jack Walker were teammates with the following Cup winners: the 1914 Toronto Blueshirts, the 1917 Seattle Metropolitans and the 1925 Victoria Cougars.

Hockey's Other Half

Women's hockey has a history that stretches back well over a century. A daughter of Lord Stanley was admired for her hockey skills in the late 1800s. The Preston Rivulettes were famous throughout Canada for their impressive winning streak during the 1930s. The women's game has greatly increased in popularity and has seen unbelievable growth in both Canada and the United States over the last two decades.

First Period— Who Am I?

1. *I am the first female goaltender to be credited with a win in a professional hockey game.*
While many people associate Manon Rheaume with professional hockey, Erin Whitten was actually the first to obtain a victory. On October 30, 1993, she replaced injured goaltender Alain Harvey of the Toledo Storm in a 1-1 tie. The game ended 6-5 in favor of Toledo, with Whitten getting the win.

2. *I have played both forward and defense for Canada from 1994 to 2002.*
Cassie Campbell played defense from 1994 to 1998, switching to forward in 1999. In 1997, at the World Championships, she was named to the All-Star Team on defense.

Geraldine Heaney, of Team Canada, played in every World Championship and Olympic competition involving women's hockey between 1990 and 2002.

3. *I played for Team Canada at the World Championships in 1990 and 1992 before becoming coach of the Swiss national team for the 1997 World Championships.*
France Montour scored eight points in five games in 1990 and seven points in 1992. Montour also played in Japan and Switzerland before taking over coaching for the Swiss national team.

4. *I was a fifteen-year-old goaltender at the 2002 Olympic Games.*
Goaltender Kim Martin played in three games for Sweden at the Salt Lake City Games. The fifteen year old had a .939 save percentage, with a 1.67 goals-against-average in her first Olympic experience.

5. *I played for Team Canada in the first three World Championships before moving on to a career in broadcasting and coaching.*
Margot Page (nee Verlaan) recorded nineteen points, with six goals and thirteen assists, during her time with Team Canada. She has since gone on to broadcast for TSN and CBC. She is also currently head coach of Niagara University's women's hockey team.

6. *I was the oldest player on the Canadian Olympic team in 1998.*
France St. Louis was thirty-nine during the Olympics in Nagano. A true veteran, during the 1990 World Championships, St. Louis was one of the older players at thirty-one years of age. When she retired in 1999, St. Louis had recorded fifty-one points in sixty-seven games during her career with the Canadian national team.

7. *I am the first goalie to be documented as wearing a mask.*
While Clint Benedict was the first NHL goalie to wear a mask, goaltender Elizabeth Graham began wearing one in 1927 while playing for Queens University. She donned a wire fencing mask three years before Clint Benedict wore a mask to protect his broken nose. It wasn't until Jacques Plante began to wear a mask in 1959 that it was again adopted routinely for protection.

8. *My number 8 was retired by the Beatrice Aeros of the NWHL in 2001.*
Angela James announced her retirement at New Years of 2001. James had an outstanding career, including four World Championships. During her international career, she recorded thirty-three goals and twenty-one assists for fifty-four points.

9. *I am the only player to join Geraldine Heaney on the winning Canadian team in both the 1990 World Championships and the 2002 Olympic Games.*
Vicky Sunohara played for Canada during the 1990 World Championships, but missed the next two tournaments in 1992 and 1994. She joined the national team again in 1997, and has won a total of five gold medals in the World Championships. Sunohara has also played on both Olympic teams, winning a gold and silver medal.

10. *I took my case all the way to the Supreme Court for the right to play on a boys' team.*

When she was first disallowed from participating on a boys' peewee team in 1985, Justine Blainey took her case to court. Her case lasted four years, during which time she appeared before the Ontario Human Rights Commission and eventually the Supreme Court of Canada. In the end, Blainey won her case, allowing her to play on a boys' team.

11. *I won a gold medal in the first World Ringette Championships and the first World Hockey Championship in 1990.*

Judy Diduck was on the Western Canadian team that defeated Ontario 3-2 in the World Ringette Championships. She was also a member of the gold medal-winning Canadian team in hockey as they defeated the United States 5-2. Diduck was a member of the Canadian national team until the year 2000.

12. *I led all those playing defense in scoring during the 2002 Winter Olympics.*

Tara Mounsey of the United States recorded seven assists to lead all blueliners in scoring. Canada's Therese Brisson finished second with two goals and three assists for five points.

13. *I scored all of my team's goals during the 1932 hockey season.*

Fran Crooks played for the University of Toronto. In 1932, they played two games against Queens. They won the first game 3-2 and tied the second 2-2. Crooks scored all five of her team's goals. In 1933, the University League was abandoned due to the Depression, at which time Crooks helped organize a team called the Toronto Vagabonds.

14. *I scored the overtime winner of the 1997 World Championships, my third goal of the game.*

Nancy Drolet was a member of Team Canada from 1992 until 2002. She scored the winning goal of the 1997 Championship game at 12:59 of the first overtime period to beat the Americans 4-3. During that tournament, Drolet recorded six points in five games, including a hat trick in the final.

15. *Although the majority of my athletic achievements have occurred in track and field, my first taste of fame was in hockey.*

Abby Hoffman played hockey during the 1955–56 season, until the Toronto Hockey League found out that she was a girl. With hockey then out of reach, Abby turned her attentions to other sports. She competed in four Olympic, four Pan-American and two Commonwealth games. Throughout her career, she won two gold medals in the Pan-Am games and one in the Commonwealth games. Her contribution to hockey, however, has not been forgotten, as a trophy in her name is presented to the winner of the Canadian National Championships. The Abby Hoffman Cup was first presented in 1982.

16. *I am the first female player to attend an NHL rookie training camp as a forward.*
Hayley Wickenheiser first attended the Philadelphia Flyers Prospect Camp in July of 1998.

17. *I was the first female head coach of the Canadian national women's team.*
Shannon Miller was the head coach of the Canadian Olympic team at the 1998 games in Nagano. She was the first person to be a full-time coach of the women's national team program.

18. *I scored the first goal in women's Olympic hockey history.*
Sari Krooks of Finland scored the first goal of the 1998 Olympics during a 6-0 win over Sweden.

19. *I am the referee who called eight consecutive penalties against the Canadian national team in the 2002 Olympic gold medal game.*
Stacey Livingston was the American referee who officiated the final game of the 2002 Olympics. She became infamous in Canada as her calls forced Team Canada to kill off eleven American power plays, including eight consecutive calls, en route to their gold medal win.

20. *I was participating in my third Olympic games at Salt Lake City in 2002.*
Hayley Wickenheiser played for the Canadian hockey team in both the 1998 and 2002 Winter Olympics. A multi-sport athlete, Wickenheiser was also a member of the Canadian softball team during the 2000 Summer Olympics in Sydney.

Second Period— Multiple Choice

1. *Who scored the winning goal in the 1990 World Championships gold medal game?*
a) Geraldine Heaney
b) Angela James
c) Laura Schuler
d) Stacy Wilson
a) Geraldine Heaney scored the winner on an end-to-end rush, often compared with Bobby Orr's famous Cup-winning goal. This goal was even featured during *Hockey Night in Canada's* top ten goals of the 1989–1990 season. Team Canada went on to win the game by a score of 5-2.

2. *When was women's hockey first included in the NHL All-Star weekend?*
a) 1996 b) 1997 c) 1998 d) 1999
c) 1998. On January 16, 1998, at the NHL All-Star weekend in Vancouver, Team Canada beat the USA 2-1.

Manon Rheame
is the only
woman to have
played in an
NHL exhibition
game to date.

3. *What is the most goals scored by a team in a gold medal World Championship game?*
a) 6   b) 8   c) 10   d) 12
b) 8. Canada defeated the United States 8-0 in the gold medal game of the 1992 World Championships held in Finland.

4. *Which country made its first appearance at the 1997 World Championships?*
a) Japan   b) Russia
c) Denmark   d) Germany
b) Russia. Although the Russian men have had a strong program for several years with much international success, the women's program is very new, with 1997 being the first time the women's team made an appearance. They finished in sixth place, missing qualifying for the 1998 Olympics by one placement. Germany and Japan first participated in the World Championships during 1990, and Denmark in 1992.

5. *How many members of Team Canada played in their first Olympic game at Salt Lake City in 2002?*
a) 7   b) 8   c) 9   d) 10
d) 10. Canada had ten players in Salt Lake City playing in their first Olympics. They were: Colleen Sostorics, Cheryl Pounder, Sami-Jo Small, Isabelle Chartrand, Caroline Ouellette, Dana Antal, Kelly Bechard, Tammy Lee Shewchuk, Cherie Piper and Kim St. Pierre.

6. *Who was in goal for the USA team when they won the gold medal in Nagano?*
a) Sara DeCosta   b) Sarah Tueting
c) Erin Whitten   d) Kelly Dyer
b) Sarah Tueting. It is a common misconception that Erin Whitten played net for the gold medal, but she never saw any game action during the Olympics. Team USA's other goalie was Sara DeCosta, who played during the Championship game in 2002. Kelly Dyer was a member of the national team from 1990 until 1995.

7. *During the season preceding the 2002 Olympics, how many times had the US defeated Canada?*
a) 6   b) 7   c) 8   d) 9
c) 8. Prior to the Olympics, Team USA had recorded eight straight wins over Canada and had an overall record of 31-0-0. They ran their record to thirty-five straight wins in the first four games of the Olympics tournament before losing to Canada in the gold medal game.

8. *How many teams participated in the women's hockey tournament in the 2002 Olympic games?*
a) 6   b) 8   c) 10   d) 12
b) 8. China, Finland, Germany, Kazakstan, Russia, Sweden, Canada and the United States all participated in women's hockey in the 2002 Salt Lake City Olympic Games.

9. *Goaltender Manon Rheaume played twenty minutes of exhibition hockey with the Tampa Bay Lightning against the St. Louis Blues on September 23, 1992. However, Rheaume also played another period of exhibition hockey for the Lightning the following year. What team did Rheaume face in her second NHL exhibition appearance?*
a) The Boston Bruins
b) The Chicago Blackhawks
c) The Detroit Red Wings
d) The New York Rangers

a) The Boston Bruins. On October 1, 1993, Rheaume played the first period against the Bruins, stopping eight of eleven shots in a 4-2 Boston win.

10. *How many countries have hosted the women's World Championships?*
a) 3   b) 4   c) 5   d) 6

a) 3. There have been seven World Championships played to the end of the 2001–02 season, with only three countries hosting the event. Canada hosted the World Championships on three occasions: 1990, 1997 and 2000. Finland held the Championship tournament in 1992 and 1999, while the USA hosted the Championships in 1994 and 2001.

11. *How many different players have served as captain of Team Canada at the World Championships and the Olympics between 1990 and 2002?*
a) 4   b) 5   c) 6   d) 7

b) 5. Sue Scherer, France St. Louis, Stacy Wilson and Therese Brisson have all served as captain of Team Canada up to 2001. Cassie Campbell was the captain of the gold medal-winning Canadian team at the 2002 Olympics.

12. *Which player did not lead the 2002 Olympic scoring race?*
a) Hayley Wickenheiser
b) Cammi Granato
c) Natalie Darwitz
d) Danielle Goyette

c) Natalie Darwitz. Wickenheiser, Granato and Goyette all tied for first place in scoring during the Olympics with ten points each. Darwitz finished in second place with eight points.

13. *The Brampton Canadettes are known for hosting the largest female hockey tournament in the world. When was it first held?*
a) 1956   b) 1967   c) 1978   d) 1982

b) 1967. In 1967, Brampton hosted twenty-two teams from Ontario. Today, over three hundred teams from all over the world take part in this famous tournament.

14. *Who was the youngest player to be a member of a gold medal-winning team at the World Championships?*
a) Cheryl Pounder
b) Caroline Ouellette
c) Kim St. Pierre
d) Hayley Wickenheiser
d) Hayley Wickenheiser was fifteen years old when she played for Canada at the 1994 World Championships in Lake Placid.

15. *My sweater number 21 is the same number worn by my brother throughout most of his NHL career.*
a) Jennifer Botterill
b) Judy Diduck
c) Cammi Granato
d) Stephanie O'Sullivan
c) Cammi Granato sports number 21 as a member of Team USA. Her brother, Tony Granato, wore number 21 in most of his thirteen NHL seasons.

16. *When was women's hockey first named as an official Olympic sport?*
a) 1992   b) 1994   c) 1996   d) 1998
b) 1994. Women's hockey was considered, but not accepted, as a sport for the 1994 Olympics in Lillehammer, Norway. Ironically, it was in 1994 that it was named as an official sport for the 1998 Olympics in Nagano, Japan.

17. *How many games has Canada lost at the first seven World Championships?*
a) 0   b) 1   c) 2   d) 3
a) 0. Canada has an incredible 35-0-0 record in the seven World Championships held between 1990 and 2001.

18. *I was the leading scorer at the Winter Olympics in 1998.*
a) Katie King
b) Danielle Goyette
c) Riika Nieminen
d) Hayley Wickenheiser
c) Riika Nieminen of Finland recorded seven goals and five assists for twelve points in six games to lead the scoring at the 1998 Olympics. Canada's Danielle Goyette finished in second place with ten points, while Katie King of the United States recorded eight points and Hayley Wickenheiser of Canada had seven points in the Olympic tournament.

19. *I wore number 33 at the World Championships in 1994 for Team Canada.*
a) Manon Rheaume
b) Marianne Grnak
c) Hayley Wickenheiser
d) Kim St. Pierre
b) Marianne Grnak. Although many people know 33 as Manon Rheaume's number, she wore 1 for the tournament while Grnak wore 33 for Team Canada in her only World Championship appearance. Kim St. Pierre currently wears number 33 but didn't join the national team until prior to the 1999 Three Nations Cup. Hayley Wickenheiser has always worn number 22 while skating for Canada.

20. *How many countries have won an Olympic medal in women's hockey?*
a) 3   b) 4   c) 5   d) 6

b) 4. Canada, United States, Finland and Sweden have all won medals in Olympic women's hockey.

1998		2002	
Medal	**Team**	**Medal**	**Team**
Gold	USA	Gold	Canada
Silver	Canada	Silver	USA
Bronze	Finland	Bronze	Sweden

Third Period—
Expert Trivia

1. *The Preston Rivulettes are well known for their remarkable record of 348 wins and two losses between 1930 and 1939. Who was the only team to beat the Rivulettes during this time?*

The Edmonton Rustlers. After defeating Toronto 1-0 to win the Eastern Championship, the Rivulettes challenged the Western Champions, Edmonton, for the first ever Dominion title. The Rivulettes lost the first game 3-2, and the second 1-0. Edmonton won the Bessborough Trophy on a two game total goal series 4-2.

2. *What color uniforms did Team Canada wear at the 1990 World Championships?*

Pink and white. Instead of the traditional red and white Canadian uniforms, the team suited up in pink uniforms with white trim in order to attract media attention. For the next World Championships, held in 1992, the women's team wore the traditional red and white.

3. *Name the three members of the Harvard University forward line that scored an incredible 307 points in 1998–99. (Hint: They all played in the 2002 Olympics.)*

Jennifer Botterill, A.J. Mleczko and Tammy Lee Shewchuk scored a record 307 points for Harvard in 1998–99. Botterill and Shewchuk were members of the gold medal-winning Canadian team, while Mleczko was a member of the silver medalists from the USA.

4. *Who was the only non-North American in the top ten scorers during the 2002 Olympic Games?*

Katja Riipi of Finland was tied for tenth place in scoring, with six points, three goals and three assists. All other players in the top ten were either a member of Team Canada or Team USA.

Cammi Granato
has represented
the United States
at all major inter-
national events
for women's
hockey from 1990
through 2002.

5. *What was the major difference regarding rule interpretation between the 1990 and 1992 World Championships?*

Although body checking was technically illegal in 1990, the rule was not enforced for fear that European teams would pull out of the tournament without it. From 1992 on, the rule has been enforced.

6. *When was the first Canadian Interuniversity Athletic Union (CIAU) National Championship held?*

Despite the fact that university hockey has been played for over one hundred years, the first CIAU Championships were held in 1998. The Concordia Stingers hosted the event in Montreal. In the championship game, the Concordia Stingers beat the Toronto Varsity Blues by a score of 4-1. Université du Quebec à Trois-Rivieres defeated the Guelph Gryphons 4-3 in overtime for the bronze medal.

7. *Which teams competed in the first official World Championships in 1990?*

The following eight countries, Canada, United States, Finland, Sweden, Switzerland, Norway, Germany and Japan, all participated in the first official World Championships in 1990.

8. *Who is the only player to join Cammi Granato on Team USA for both the 1990 World Championships and 2002 Olympics?*

Sue Merz and Cammi Granato are the only two players to represent the United States in both of these tournaments.

9. *Name the only two individuals to have coached a gold medal-winning team in women's hockey at the Olympics.*

Ben Smith was appointed head coach of Team USA in June of 1996. In 1998, he coached the United States to their gold medal Olympic victory. Daniele Sauvageau's first stint as head coach occurred during the 1998–1999 season. She then took some time away from the national team program before returning to coach the Canadian women to their first gold medal in Olympic hockey in Salt Lake City.

10. *There has been controversy in both 1998 and 2002 regarding a player left off the Canadian women's Olympic hockey team. Can you name the players?*

In 1998, there was considerable controversy when Angela James was cut from the Canadian Olympic hockey team. Nancy Drolet missed the Olympics when replaced in favor of youngster Cherie Piper for the 2002 games at Salt Lake City. Both players appealed but lost, excluding them from the Olympic team.

11. *Who are the only two individuals to have ever scored the winning goal in a gold medal women's hockey match at the Olympics?*

In 2002, Jayna Hefford scored at 19:59 of the second period to give Canada a 3-1 lead. Canada held on for a 3-2 victory over the United States to claim the gold medal. In 1998, at Nagano, Shelley Looney scored at 10:59 of the third period to give the United States a 2-1 lead. They would go on to win by a final score of 3-1.

12. *Name the four Canadian players who participated in four World Championships and the Olympics between 1990 and 1998.*
Judy Diduck, Geraldine Heaney, France St. Louis and Stacy Wilson. Heaney had been the longest serving member of the national team when she retired after the 2002 Olympics.

13. *Where did Daniele Sauvageau coach between her appointments as head coach of Team Canada?*
Daniele Sauvageau was an assistant coach with the Montreal Rockets of the Quebec Major Junior Hockey League during the 1999–2000 season. The Quebec Major Junior Hockey League is one of three Canadian junior leagues which supply numerous players to the National Hockey League.

14. *Name the only two Canadian goalies to play in a gold medal Olympic game.*
Manon Rheaume was in net for the Canadian silver medalists in the final game of the 1998 Olympics. Canada's Kim St. Pierre led her team to a gold medal against the Americans in the 2002 Winter Olympics.

15. *Name the only female winners of the prestigious Lester Patrick Trophy.*
The Lester Patrick Trophy, which is presented for outstanding service to hockey in the United States, was presented to the US Olympic women's hockey team in 1999 for their gold medal-winning performance in the 1998 Winter Olympics.

16. *What member of the 2002 Canadian Olympic team had a mother participate in earlier Olympic games?*
Jennifer Botterill's mother Doreen participated in both the 1964 and 1968 Winter Olympics as a speed skater. Botterill comes from a sports family. Her father is a sports psychologist and her brother Jason has skated in the NHL with several teams.

17. *Which states were home to the most members of the 2002 US Olympic team?*
Massachusetts, Minnesota, New Hampshire and New York were each represented by three players on the silver medal-winning US Olympic team of 2002.

18. *Name two veterans at the 2002 Olympics who first represented the United States at the 1992 World Championships.*
Karyn Bye and Shelley Looney first saw action with the US national team at the 1992 World Championships in Finland.

19. *What number did Geraldine Heaney wear throughout her playing career with the Canadian national team?*
Canada's Geraldine Heaney wore number 91 in all international tournaments from 1990 to 2002.

20. *How many women have been inducted into the Hockey Hall of Fame?*
There have been no women selected for membership into the Hockey Hall of Fame to date; however, it should only be a matter of time before such recognition will take place.

Connections

Hockey is a team game; it cannot be won by a single individual. The members of the various hockey organizations have, over the years, formed the foundations of this great sport. By relying on peers and family, the individual player achieves more through the connections made. Can you identify the ties that have made hockey history?

First Period— Teammates

1. *Who were the only two members of Team USA in the 2002 Olympics not born in the United States?*
Two members of Team USA were actually born in Canada. Brett Hull was born in Belleville, Ontario, and Adam Deadmarsh in Trail, British Columbia.

2. *Name the only two players to have been members of Stanley Cup-winning teams with both the Edmonton Oilers and the Montreal Canadiens.*
Pat Hughes and Mark Napier. Pat Hughes skated with both the 1979 Montreal Canadiens and the 1984 and 1985 Stanley Cup champion Edmonton Oilers. Mark Napier was a teammate on both the 1979 Montreal Canadiens and the 1985 Edmonton Oilers.

3. *When Chicago won the Stanley Cup in 1961, it marked the only time between 1956 and 1969 that a team other than Montreal or Toronto took the Cup. However, two members of the 1961 Black Hawks would include this victory in a string of four consecutive Cups.*
Can you name these two players?
Ab McDonald and Eddie Litzenberger. Ab McDonald had won the Cup with Montreal in 1958, 1959 and 1960. After the Stanley Cup victory in 1961, Eddie Litzenberger was a member of the Stanley Cup-winning teams in Toronto in 1962, 1963 and 1964.

There were other 1961 Black Hawks with connections to the Montreal and Toronto cup winners between 1956 and 1969. Dollard St. Laurent was with the Montreal Cup winners of 1956, 1957 and

1958, while Al Arbour would join Litzenberger on the Leaf winners in 1962 and 1964.

The 1961 Black Hawks also included Reg Fleming and Murray Balfour, who had made brief appearances with Montreal during previous Cup-winning seasons, but had not had their names engraved on the Cup as members of the Canadiens.

4. *Name the seven players who were teammates on Cup-winning teams in Edmonton in 1990 and the Rangers in 1994.*

Glenn Anderson, Jeff Beukeboom, Adam Graves, Kevin Lowe, Craig MacTavish, Mark Messier and Esa Tikkanen all skated for both of these Cup-winning teams.

5. *Name the two teams who could boast two former Norris Trophy winners in their lineups for the 2001–02 NHL season.*

Both Chris Chelios and Nicklas Lidstrom of the Detroit Red Wings have been Norris Trophy winners, while the St. Louis Blues have former Norris Trophy winners Chris Pronger and Al MacInnis on their roster.

6. *Name the two individuals who were teammates on both the Ottawa Senators' last Cup-winning club as well as the first Maple Leaf Cup winners.*

King Clancy and Frank Finnigan were members of the Senators' Cup-winning team in 1927. Clancy was then purchased by the Leafs in a trade in 1930. When the Senators suspended operations, Finnigan was loaned to the Leafs for the 1931–32 season, the year Toronto won their first Stanley Cup as the Leafs.

7. *Name the two members of the 1934 Chicago Black Hawks who died during the off-season.*

The 1933–34 Chicago Black Hawks won the first Stanley Cup championship for that city. However, tragically, the team lost two members prior to the beginning of the following season. All-Star goaltender Charlie Gardiner died of a brain hemorrhage in his hometown of Winnipeg in June of 1934. Rookie forward Jack Leswick, who had only seen seven games of NHL action the previous season, tragically drowned in August of 1934.

8. *Who were the only NHL teammates to both be named to the 2002 Olympic All-Star Team?*

Goalie Mike Richter and defenseman Brian Leetch of the New York Rangers and Team USA were both named to the 2002 Olympic All-Star Team. The other All-Stars were forwards John Leclair of the Flyers with Team USA, Joe Sakic of the Avalanche with Canada, and Mats Sundin of the Leafs with Sweden, as well as Red Wing Chris Chelios of Team USA on defense.

9. *Name the three players, who went on to become Hall of Famers, who saw their last NHL action with the Montreal Canadiens in 1978–79.*

The Montreal Canadiens won their fourth straight Cup title in 1979. Jacques Lemaire, who scored the Stanley Cup-winning goal, and goalie Ken Dryden ended their careers after this championship win. Captain Yvan Cournoyer also saw his last NHL action as a member of this club, having only played fifteen games during the 1978–79 season due to injury. Cournoyer had back surgery in December 1978 and was later forced to retire as a result of his back problems.

10. *Name the six players who were members of the Colorado Avalanche Stanley Cup champion teams in both 1996 and 2001.*
Adam Foote, Peter Forsberg, Jon Klemm, Patrick Roy, Joe Sakic and Stephane Yelle were members of the Colorado Cup winners in both of these seasons.

11. *Name the four members of the 1991 Stanley Cup champion Pittsburgh Penguins who had been a member of the first Stanley Cup victory of other NHL franchises.*
Brian Trottier had been a member of the 1980 New York Islanders, Paul Coffey of the 1984 Edmonton Oilers, and Joe Mullen and Jiri Hrdina of the 1989 Calgary Flames.

12. *What two members of the Canadian Olympic team in 2002 had been involved in a trade for each other in the 1995 NHL season?*
Joe Nieuwendyk was traded by Calgary to Dallas in return for Jarome Iginla in December of 1995. Corey Millen accompanied Iginla to Calgary in the trade.

13. *Name the two superstars who both played their final NHL game as teammates during the 1980 Stanley Cup playoffs.*
Gordie Howe and Bobby Hull, both as members of the Hartford Whalers, saw their final NHL action on April 11, 1980, as the Whalers lost 4-3 in overtime to the Montreal Canadiens.

14. *Name the last three Canadian-born winners of the Calder Trophy prior to the 2001–02 NHL season. (Hint: All three of these players were members of Canada's 2002 Olympic team.)*
Joe Nieuwendyk of the Calgary Flames in 1988, Ed Belfour of the Chicago Blackhawks in 1991 and Martin Brodeur of the New Jersey Devils in 1994 were the last three Canadian-born winners of the Calder Trophy as the NHL's rookie of the year prior to Canadian Dany Heatley being awarded the Calder for his performance during the 2001–02 NHL season.

15. *Name the first round selection of the Atlanta Thrashers in each of the first three NHL entry drafts they participated in.*
The Thrashers selected Patrik Stefan, who was picked first overall in the 1999 entry draft. They followed this up by selecting Dany Heatley second overall in the 2000 draft and Ilya Kovalchuk first overall in the 2001 entry draft.

16. *Name the three individuals who served as captain of the St. Louis Blues during the 1995–96 NHL season.*
Brett Hull, Shayne Corson and Wayne Gretzky all served as captain of the St. Louis Blues during the 1995–96 season.

17. *Name the four Hall of Famers that were NHL goaltending partners of Ed Johnston.*
Gerry Cheevers shared the Bruin net with Johnston from 1965–66 until his departure to the WHA for the 1972–73 season. Bernie Parent tended goal with both Cheevers and Johnston for the first two of these

Goaltender Ed Johnston was a steady performer throughout his sixteen NHL seasons.

seasons, until being claimed by Philadelphia in the 1967 expansion draft. Jacques Plante arrived in a trade from Toronto to join Johnston in Boston near the end of the 1972–73 season. Johnston moved on to Toronto and St. Louis before ending his playing career as a backup for Tony Esposito with Chicago in 1978.

18. *Name the two Team USA teammates at the 2002 Olympics who were involved in the same trade shortly after the Olympic games.*
Olympian Mike York was traded by the New York Rangers to the Edmonton Oilers, with Team USA teammate Tom Poti going the other way in a trade less than a month after the Salt Lake City Games. Rem Murray accompanied Poti to the Rangers in the deal.

19. *Name the only three players to have their numbers retired by the Hartford Whalers. They were teammates on the New England Whalers during the final two WHA seasons.*
Rick Ley, Gordie Howe and Johnny McKenzie had numbers 2, 9 and 19, respectively, retired by the Hartford Whalers. Since the franchise was relocated to Carolina as the Hurricanes, only Howe's number 9 has not been worn.

20. *Name the two sets of brothers who were teammates on Team Canada '72.*
Phil and Tony Esposito and Frank and Peter Mahovlich competed for Canada in the 1972 Summit Series against the Soviet Union.

Second Period — What's the Link?

1. *Theo Fleury, Ray Bourque, Joe Nieuwendyk, Eric Lindros, Brendan Shanahan*
These are the five shooters that Dominik Hasek stopped in the shootout of the semi-final game at the 1998 Olympic Games. Hasek's heroics gave the Czech Republic a 2-1 win over Canada en route to the gold medal at the games held in Nagano, Japan.

2. *Howie Morenz, Toe Blake, Jean Beliveau, Henri Richard, Jacques Lemaire*
All of these Hall of Famers scored two Stanley Cup-winning goals for the Montreal Canadiens: Howie Morenz in 1924 and 1930, Toe Blake in 1944 and 1946, Jean Beliveau in 1960 and 1965, Henri Richard in 1966 and 1971, and Jacques Lemaire in 1977 and 1979.

3. *Dan Cloutier, Chris Osgood, Dominik Hasek, Arturs Irbe*
All of these goalies wore cage-style face masks during the 2001–02 NHL season.

4. *Lionel Conacher, Red Dutton, Ching Johnson, Al Shields, Eddie Shore*

These five individuals skated on defense the first time the NHL iced an All-Star time.

The Ace Bailey Benefit Game was played on Wednesday, February 14, 1934, at Maple Leaf Gardens. The game was staged to raise funds for injured Maple Leaf forward, Ace Bailey, who had suffered a career-ending injury when checked by Eddie Shore in a game earlier in the season. The Toronto Maple Leafs defeated the NHL All-Stars in a game that raised over $20,000 for Ace Bailey and his family. Each of the NHL's then eight franchises (other than Toronto) were represented by two players on the NHL's All-Star Team.

Henri Richards and Bobby Hull chase the puck during a game played on December 4, 1960.

1934 All-Stars/Ace Bailey Benefit Game	
Team	**Players**
Boston Bruins	Eddie Shore—defense, Nels Stewart—forward
Chicago Black Hawks	Lionel Conacher—defense, Charlie Gardiner—goaltender
Detroit Red Wings	Larry Aurie—forward, Herbie Lewis—forward
Montreal Canadiens	Aurel Joliat—forward, Howie Morenz—forward
Montreal Maroons	Hooley Smith—forward, Jimmy Ward—forward
Ottawa Senators	Frank Finnigan—forward, Al Shields—defense
New York Americans	Red Dutton—defense, Normie Himes—forward
New York Rangers	Bill Cook—forward, Ching Johnson—defense, Lester Patrick—coach

5. *Zdeno Chara, Chris McAllister, Steve McKenna*
These are the three tallest players to play in the NHL during the 2001–02 NHL season. Defenseman Zdeno Chara of the Ottawa Senators is the tallest player in the league at 6 foot 9, while Philadelphia defenseman Chris McAllister and New York Ranger forward Steve McKenna are both 6 foot 8 inches.

6. *Charlie Gardiner, Davey Kerr, Bill Durnan, Tony Esposito, Gilles Villemure, Tom Barrasso, Grant Fuhr, Jose Theodore*
These individuals are Vezina Trophy winners who have caught the puck with their right hand.

Right-Handed Catching Vezina Trophy Winners	
Charlie Gardiner, Chicago Black Hawks	1932, 1934
Davey Kerr, New York Rangers	1940
Bill Durnan,* Montreal Canadiens	1944, 1945, 1946, 1947, 1949, 1950
Tony Esposito, Chicago Black Hawks	1970, 1972, 1974
Gilles Villemure, New York Rangers	1971
Tom Barrasso, Buffalo Sabres	1984
Grant Fuhr, Edmonton Oilers	1988
Jose Theodore, Montreal Canadiens	2002

*Durnan was listed as catching with his right, but was ambidextrous and often caught the puck with his left hand as well.

7. *Lorne Chabot, Terry Sawchuk, Jacques Plante, Gary Smith, Pete Peeters*
These individuals were established NHL goaltenders when they had a Vezina Trophy-winning season with a team they had never previously played on.

Goalie	Team	Vezina Trophy Season
Lorne Chabot	Chicago Black Hawks	1934–35
Terry Sawchuk	Toronto Maple Leafs	1964–65
Jacques Plante	St. Louis Blues	1968–69
Gary Smith	Chicago Black Hawks	1971–72
Pete Peeters	Boston Bruins	1982–83

8. *Toe Blake, Ralph Backstrom, Joe Carveth, Floyd Curry*
These four were the only players to wear number 6 for the Montreal Canadiens for over thirty seasons, from the late 1930s to the early 1970s. Toe Blake began wearing number 6 in the 1937–38 season, wearing it until his retirement due to injury in 1948. Joe Carveth then donned the number for 1948–49 and the beginning of the 1949–50 season, when the number was passed on to Floyd Curry. Curry wore it through the end of 1957–58. Ralph Backstrom wore number 6 in 1958–59 until his trade to Los Angeles in the 1970–71 season.

9. *Kenora, Seattle, Victoria*
These cities have all had teams win the Stanley Cup, but have never had a team in the National Hockey League. The Kenora Thistles won the Cup in 1907, the Seattle Metropolitans in 1917 and the Victoria Cougars in 1925.

10. *Claude Lemieux, Mario Lemieux, Patrick Roy, Steve Yzerman*
All of these Conn Smythe winners were born in 1965, the first year that the trophy was presented. In fact, Mario Lemieux and Patrick Roy share the same birthday, October 5, 1965.

11. *Joe Millar, Alfie Moore, Earl Robertson*
Each of these goalies played in the finals for a Stanley Cup-winning team without ever making an NHL regular season appearance with that franchise. Joe Millar played 127 regular season NHL games with the New York Americans, Pittsburgh Pirates and Philadelphia Quakers, but saw his only playoff action in the league as a replacement goalie for the injured Lorne Chabot during the final three games of the 1928 Stanley Cup finals versus the Montreal Maroons. Earl Robertson backstopped 190 regular season and 9 playoff games with the Americans, playing with the Detroit Red Wings for only six games during their 1937 Cup-winning playoffs. Alfie Moore saw limited action over three NHL seasons with the Americans and Red Wings, but made a single appearance with the Black Hawks in game two of their 1938 Cup-winning final series.

12. *Dave Balon, Bob Baun, Glenn Hall, Leon Rochefort, Ken Schinkel, Terry Sawchuk*
These players were selected to represent the six expansion teams for the NHL All-Stars in the 1968 All-Star Game. The defending Stanley Cup champion Toronto Maple Leafs defeated the NHL All-Stars by a score of 4-3 in the final game of this format on January 16, 1968.

Player	Team
Dave Balon	Minnesota North Stars
Bob Baun	Oakland Seals
Glenn Hall	St. Louis Blues
Leon Rochefort	Philadelphia Flyers
Ken Schinkel	Pittsburgh Penguins
Terry Sawchuk	Los Angeles Kings

13. *Benoit Brunet, Benoit Hogue, Martin Rucinsky, Darren Van Impe*
All four of these players played for three different teams during the 2001–02 NHL season. Van Impe saw game action with the Rangers, Panthers and Islanders, while Hogue suited up with Dallas, Boston and Washington. Both Rucinsky and Brunet played for Montreal and Dallas, with Rucinsky going on to the Rangers and Brunet going on to the Senators.

14. *Anders Hedberg, Bobby Hull, Andre Lacroix, Paul Shmyr, Marc Tardif, J.C. Tremblay*
These are the only six players to be chosen as members of the WHA's First All-Star Team on three separate occasions. J.C. Tremblay, of the Quebec Nordiques, was chosen on defense in 1972–73, 1974–75 and 1975–76. Paul Shmyr was selected as a member from the Cleveland Crusaders in 1972–73, 1973–74 and 1975–76. Winnipeg Jet Bobby Hull made the team for the WHA's first three seasons, 1972–73 through 1974–75. Andre Lacroix, of Philadelphia/New York/New Jersey/San Diego, was named to the All-Star Team at center during the same three seasons. Marc Tardif was chosen as left wing from the Quebec Nordiques during the seasons from 1975–76 through 1977–78. Anders Hedberg, of the Winnipeg Jets, was honored as an All-Star in three consecutive seasons from 1975–76 to 1977–78.

15. *Chris Chelios, Igor Kravchuk, Brian Leetch, Jyrki Lumme, Teppo Numminen, Scott Young*

These 2001–02 NHL players all participated in the Olympic games in the 1980s, the 1990s, and again in 2002.

Player	Country	Olympic Years
Chris Chelios	United States	1984, 1998, 2002
Igor Kravchuk	Soviet Union, Russia	1988, 1992, 1998, 2002
Brian Leetch	United States	1988, 1998, 2002
Jyrki Lumme	Finland	1988, 1998, 2002
Teppo Numminen	Finland	1988, 1998, 2002
Scott Young	United States	1988, 1992, 2002

16. *Steve Duchesne, Peter Forsberg, Ron Hextall, Kerry Huffman, Mike Ricci, Chris Simon*

The Quebec Nordiques received these six players in return for trading the rights to Eric Lindros to the Philadelphia Flyers on June 30, 1992. The Nordiques also received $15,000 and two first round picks for the 1993 and 1994 entry drafts in the deal. They selected Jocelyn Thibault with the 1993 selection, while including the other first round pick in their major trade with the Toronto Maple Leafs at the 1994 entry draft.

17. *Gerry Cheevers, Ken Dryden, Tony Esposito, Grant Fuhr, George Hainsworth, Andy Moog, Jacques Plante, Terry Sawchuk*

These retired NHL goalies all won at least one hundred more regular season games than they lost.

	Wins	Losses	Difference	(Ties)
Ken Dryden	258	57	201	(74)
Jacques Plante	435	247	188	(145)
Andy Moog	372	209	163	(88)
Gerry Cheevers	230	102	128	(74)
Tony Esposito	423	306	117	(151)
Terry Sawchuk	446	332	114	(171)
Grant Fuhr	403	295	108	(114)
George Hainsworth	246	145	101	(74)

18. *Eric Brewer, Zdeno Chara, Darius Kasparaitis, Scott Lachance, Bryan McCabe, Wade Redden*

These six NHL defensemen were all originally selected by the New York Islanders in the NHL entry draft.

Defensemen Selected by the New York Islanders in NHL Entry Drafts			
Entry Draft Selection	Selected Overall	Player	2001–02 Team
1991	4	Scott Lachance	Vancouver Canucks
1992	5	Darius Kasparaitis	Pittsburgh Penguins, Colorado Avalanche
1993	40	Bryan McCabe	Toronto Maple Leafs
1995	2	Wade Redden	Ottawa Senators
1996	56	Zdeno Chara	Ottawa Senators
1997	5	Eric Brewer	Edmonton Oilers

19. *Jim Rutherford, Greg Millen, Sean Burke, Kirk McLean*

All four of these goalies appeared with three different NHL teams in one season. Jim Rutherford made appearances in 1980–81 with Detroit, Toronto and Los Angeles. Greg Millen was next in 1989–90 when he played for St. Louis, Quebec and Chicago. Sean Burke and Kirk McLean both duplicated the feat in 1997–98: Burke with Carolina, Vancouver and Philadelphia and McLean with Carolina, Vancouver and Florida.

20. *Cy Denneny, Dit Clapper, Ted Lindsay, Stan Mikita, Mark Messier*

At least one of these five individuals played in each of the first eighty-five seasons of the NHL. At each "link" there is at least one season where both players saw NHL action.

Player	NHL Seasons	Teams
Cy Denneny	1917–18 to 1927–28	Ottawa Senators, Boston Bruins
Dit Clapper	1927–28 to 1946–47	Boston Bruins
Ted Lindsay	1944–45 to 1959–60, 1964–65	Detroit Red Wings, Chicago Black Hawks
Stan Mikita	1958–59 to 1979–80	Chicago Black Hawks
Mark Messier	1979–80 to 2001–02	Edmonton, New York Rangers, Vancouver

Third Period— Family Ties

1. *Name the only two father and son combinations where both the father and the son have finished in the top ten in NHL scoring sometime in their career.*

Syl Apps Sr. and Jr. and Bobby and Brett Hull. Syl Apps Sr. finished in the top ten of scoring on six different occasions in 1936–37, 1937–38, 1938–39, 1940–41, 1941–42 and in his final season in 1947–48, all as a member of the Toronto Maple Leafs. Syl Apps Jr. achieved the same feat on two occasions in 1973–74 and 1975–76, both times as a member of the Pittsburgh Penguins. Bobby Hull finished in the top ten on eleven different occasions, in 1959–60, every season from 1961–62 through 1968–69, in 1970–71 and in 1971–72, all as a member of the Chicago Black Hawks. His son, Brett, maintained a top ten placement in the scoring race in three consecutive seasons, from 1989–90 to 1991–92, all as a member of the St. Louis Blues.

2. *This 2001–02 NHL rookie from Finland had a father who played in the league.*

Forward Niklas Hagman recorded twenty-eight points in seventy-eight games with the Florida Panthers in his rookie season. His father, Matti Hagman, recorded six points in five games as Finland's leading scorer in the 1976 Canada Cup. He went on to play in the 1976–77 and 1977–78 seasons with the Boston Bruins, and finished the 1977–78 season with the Quebec Nordiques of the WHA. He then played in the NHL as a member of the Edmonton Oilers for the 1980–81 and 1981–82 seasons. Matti Hagman also participated for Finland in the 1981 and 1987 Canada Cups.

3. *Name the first three sets of twins to have played in the NHL.*

When Daniel and Henrik Sedin hit the ice with the Vancouver Canucks for the 2000–01 season, they joined Rich and Ron Sutter, Patrik and Peter Sundstrom and Peter and Chris Ferraro as the only twins to have played in the NHL.

4. *Who were the first father and son to be elected to the Hockey Hall of Fame?*

Oliver and Earl Seibert are the first father and son to both receive such an honor. Oliver was an outstanding forward playing for Berlin (now Kitchener), Guelph and Sault Ste. Marie in the early days of organized hockey in Ontario. His son, Earl, played defense with the Rangers, Black Hawks and Red Wings between 1931–32 and 1945–46. Earl was elected to the First or Second Annual All-Star Team in ten of his fifteen NHL seasons. Oliver was selected for the Hall of Fame in 1961, while Earl followed his father into the Hall two years later.

5. *Who were the first brothers to play on the same team in an NHL All-Star game and play against each other in the next All-Star game?*
Doug and Max Bentley of the Chicago Black Hawks were teammates on the NHL All-Stars on October 13, 1947. The Toronto Maple Leafs defeated the All-Stars in the First Annual All-Star Classic. Max Bentley was traded to the Leafs shortly after in November of 1947. Max then suited up for Toronto in the Second Annual Game while brother Doug again played for the All-Stars who defeated the Leafs 3-1 in Chicago on November 3, 1948.

6. *Name the two Hall of Fame brothers who have coached consecutive Canadian entries in the Olympic Winter Games.*
Former Bruins star Bobby Bauer coached the Kitchener-Waterloo Dutchmen as they represented Canada at both the 1956 and 1960 Olympic Winter Games. His brother, Father David Bauer, then organized and coached Canada's national team for the 1964 Olympic Winter Games.

Daniel and Henrik Sedin are the fourth twins to play in the NHL.

7. *Who were the first brothers to face each other as opposing player and goalie in the NHL?*

Paul Thompson was a third year forward with the New York Rangers when goaltending brother Cecil, better known as "Tiny," joined the Boston Bruins for the 1928–29 season. They first faced each other in NHL action on December 4, 1928, when Tiny recorded a shutout in a 2-0 victory over the visiting Rangers. Tiny Thompson went on to backstop the Bruins to a two game sweep of brother Paul's New York Rangers in the 1929 Stanley Cup finals.

8. *As of the end of the 2001–02 season, what father and son goaltending combination has made the most career NHL appearances?*

There have been only four father and son combinations among NHL goalies: Sam and Pete LoPresti, Dennis and Pat Riggin, Ron and John Grahame, and Bob and Brent Johnson. While both John Grahame and Brent Johnson are active NHLers, Dennis and Pat Riggin have combined for the most NHL appearances through to the end of the 2001–02 season. Dennis appeared in a total of 18 regular season games in 1959–60 and 1962–63, while Pat played 350 regular-season and 25 playoff games in the late 1970s and 1980s for a combined total of 393 NHL games.

9. *Name the two brothers who faced each other in the 2002 Olympic Winter Games.*

Robert Reichel skated for the Czech Republic, while brother Martin Reichel played for Germany. The Czech Republic opened the championship round of the hockey tournament with a 8-2 victory over Germany.

10. *Name the father and son who have both tended the nets for Canada in the Olympics.*

Denis Brodeur was a member of the Kitchener-Waterloo Dutchmen who represented Canada at the 1956 Olympic Winter Games in Cortina d'Ampezzo, Italy. Brodeur had a record of three wins and one loss with a 2.00 goals-against average for the bronze medal-winning Canadian team. His son Martin had a 4-0-1 record with a GAA of 1.80, winning the gold medal with the Canadian team at Salt Lake City in 2002.

11. *This individual wore number 27 during his NHL career. His son now skates in the NHL donning his father's sweater number in reverse, number 72.*

Gilles Meloche, wearing number 27, tended goal for eighteen different seasons in the 1970s and 1980s with Chicago, California, Cleveland, Minnesota and Pittsburgh. His son, Erik Meloche, wore number 72 as a rookie with the Pittsburgh Penguins in the 2001–02 season.

12. *Name the two sets of brothers who saw game action with the New York Islanders in the 1980–81 season.*

Both Denis and Jean Potvin and Brent and Duane Sutter played for the Islanders during the 1980–81 season. Jean Potvin also joined his brother Denis on the Islanders in the previous season, while Brent became a regular with brother Duane at the beginning of 1981–82.

13. *Name the only father and son combination to have won both the Lady Byng and the Hart trophies.*
Bobby Hull won both the Hart Trophy as the NHL's most valuable player and the Lady Byng as the NHL's most gentlemanly player as a member of the Chicago Black Hawks in 1965, and again received the Hart Trophy in 1966. His son, Brett, received the Lady Byng in 1990 and the Hart Trophy in 1991 as a member of the St. Louis Blues.

14. *Name the only two sets of brothers to lead the NHL in scoring.*
Doug Bentley led the NHL in scoring in 1942–43 and was followed by his brother, Max, who led the league in scoring in two consecutive seasons, in 1945–46 and 1946–47. The Bentley brothers both played for Chicago during their league-leading seasons. Charlie Conacher of the Maple Leafs had led the league in scoring in 1933–34 and 1934–35 and was joined by his brother Roy who led the league in scoring in 1948–49 as a member of the Chicago Black Hawks. No other brothers have both led the league in scoring to date.

15. *Name the three brothers who began the 2001–02 season as head coaches of NHL teams.*
Three of the Sutter brothers all began the 2001–02 season as head NHL coaches. Darryl returned for his fifth season behind the San Jose bench, while Brian began the season as the new head coach of the Chicago Blackhawks. Duane had been named interim coach of the Florida Panthers during the 2000–01 season and began 2001–02 as the head coach, but was replaced by Mike Keenan during the season.

16. *This player was voted MVP in his only All-Star NHL game appearance in 1975. He played ten seasons in the NHL, the same number as his Hall of Fame father.*
Syl Apps Jr. had a ten year NHL career from 1970–71 to 1979–80 as a member of the New York Rangers, Pittsburgh Penguins and Los Angeles Kings. He scored two goals in his lone NHL All-Star game appearance when the Wales Conference defeated the Campbell Conference 7-1 in the 1975 game at the Montreal Forum on Tuesday, January 25. He was a steady performer throughout most of the 1970s, twice finishing in the top ten scoring, including a career high of ninety-nine points in 1975–76 as a member of the Pittsburgh Penguins. It is interesting to note that Syl Apps Sr. was the outstanding player in what could be considered his first NHL All-Star game appearance. He participated in the Babe Siebert Memorial Game on October 29, 1939, in which the NHL All-Stars faced the Montreal Canadiens. He recorded one goal and three assists in the All-Stars 5-2 victory. He recorded a goal and an assist in his only other NHL All-Star appearance on October 13, 1947.

17. *Who were the only two brothers to have both captained a Stanley Cup-winning team in the National Hockey League?*
Maurice "Rocket" Richard captained four Cup-winning Canadien teams from 1956–57 through 1959–60. His brother, Henri, was captain of the Canadiens when they won the Cup in 1972–73.

18. *Name the brothers who played on Philadelphia's first two Stanley Cup winners.*

Joe and Jimmy Watson both played defense for the 1974 and 1975 Philadelphia Flyers.

19. *How many sets of three brothers have played together on the same NHL team?*

Three sets of three brothers have played as teammates in the NHL. Reg Bentley joined brothers Doug and Max for eleven games on the 1942–43 Chicago Black Hawks. Bill Plager made appearances with St. Louis in each of the four seasons between 1968–69 and 71–72, joining his brothers, Barclay and Bob, both of whom had extensive careers with the Blues. Marian Stastny teamed up with brothers Anton and Peter on the Quebec Nordiques for the 1981–82 season. The Stastny brothers were teammates for four seasons until Marian signed with Toronto in 1985.

20. *How many sets of brothers have been named to the First All-Star Team in the same NHL season?*

Three sets of brothers have been First Team All-Stars in the same season. Lionel and Charlie Conacher were the first to share such an honor. Lionel of the Black Hawks was selected on defense and Charlie of the Maple Leafs was named at right wing on the 1933–34 First All-Star Team. The Thompson brothers followed in the 1937–38 season, as goaltender "Tiny" of the Bruins and left winger Paul of the Black Hawks were both selected as the best at their positions. Phil and Tony Esposito were together twice as members of the First All-Star Team. Goaltender Tony, of Chicago, and center Phil from Boston were named to the team in both 1969–70 and 1971–72.

Number Games

Numbers sometimes take on huge importance for followers of the game. Ninety-nine is equated with Wayne Gretzky throughout the hockey world. A fifty-goal season is recognized as a noteworthy milestone. How many of these hockey numbers are significant to you?

First Period— Prime Numbers

1. *What was the highest sweater number worn in the NHL in 2001–02?*
Jeremy Roenick wore number 97 while playing for the Philadelphia Flyers.

2. *Name the three Hall of Fame defensemen to have the number 2 retired in their honor.*
The number 2 has been retired by the Boston Bruins for Eddie Shore, by the Montreal Canadiens for Doug Harvey and by the Buffalo Sabres to honor Tim Horton.

3. *Name the players who wore number 3 for Canada and the United States in the 2002 Olympics.*
Eric Brewer of Canada and Brian Rafalski of the United States both wore number 3 for their respective teams at the 2002 Olympic Games.

4. *What number did Bobby Orr wear in his first NHL All-Star game?*
Orr didn't don his famous number 4 in an All-Star game until his third appearance in the 1970 classic. Jean Beliveau, who wore number 4, was a member of the first two NHL All-Star teams that Orr participated on. Orr wore number five 5 the 1968 NHL All-Star Game in Toronto, and number 2 in the 1969 NHL All-Star Game in Montreal.

5. *Name the five defensemen wearing number 3 in the Atlantic Division at the close of the 2001–02 season.*

Ken Daneyko of the New Jersey Devils, Dan McGillis of the Philadelphia Flyers, Tom Poti of the New York Rangers, Adrian Aucoin of the New York Islanders and Jamie Pushor of the Pittsburgh Penguins were all wearing sweater number 3 while playing defense for the five teams of the Atlantic Division.

6. *How many NHL head coaches of the 2001–02 season have an NHL sweater retired in their honor?*

Two. The Philadelphia Flyers have retired the number 7, which was worn by head coach Bill Barber. Chicago head coach Brian Sutter's number 11 has been retired by the St. Louis Blues.

7. *What is the most common retired number in the National Hockey League?*

The number 7 has been retired by the following eight NHL franchises to recognize the contributions of these players: Boston Bruins, Phil Esposito; Buffalo Sabres, Rick Martin; Dallas Stars, Neil Broten; Detroit Red Wings, Ted Lindsay; Montreal Canadiens, Howie Morenz; New York Rangers, Rod Gilbert; Philadelphia Flyers, Bill Barber; and Washington Capitals, Yvon Labre. The Toronto Maple Leafs have also honored, but not retired, number 7 to recognize the contributions of King Clancy and Tim Horton to the organization.

8. *What number did the Minnesota North Stars retire to honor Bill Masterton?*

Masterton's number 19 was retired by the Minnesota North Stars (now Dallas Stars). While he is commonly pictured wearing number 25 in his pre-season photo, Masterton donned number 19 for the Stars in his only NHL season. Masterton suffered a head injury in a game against the Oakland Seals on January 13, 1968. He passed away as a result of the injury two days later and remains the only player to have died as a result of an injury in an NHL game. The Bill Masterton Memorial Trophy has been awarded since the 1967–68 season to the "NHL player who best exemplifies the qualities of perseverance, sportsmanship and dedication to hockey."

9. *What is the highest sweater number to have been worn by a winner of the Frank J. Selke Trophy?*

Doug Gilmore of the Toronto Maple Leafs wore number 93 when he won the Selke Trophy as the best defensive forward in the NHL for the 1992–93 season.

10. *Name the player honored with the retirement of his sweater number 3 while never seeing any NHL action with that franchise.*

The Quebec Nordiques retired number 3 to honor J.C. Tremblay, who had been a member of the Quebec Nordiques in the WHA for seven seasons, from 1972 to 1979. Tremblay retired prior to the Nordiques' joining the NHL for the 1979–80 season. Tremblay had had an outstanding NHL career as a member of the Montreal Canadiens prior to joining the Nordiques in 1972.

Ken Dryden assumes his classic pose in the Canadiens' net.

11. *Name the only two players to have worn sweater number 11 for the Vancouver Canucks.*

Wayne Maki wore number 11 for the Canucks during the first two and a half years that the franchise was in the NHL. Maki was diagnosed with cancer midway through the 1972–73 season, which eventually took his life in 1974. While his number has never been officially retired by the Canucks, the only player to wear sweater number 11 since Maki was Mark Messier, who donned his trademark number 11 during his three seasons with the Canucks between 1997 and 2000.

12. *What was the first number worn by Jean Beliveau in the NHL?*

Beliveau wore number 17 in his first two NHL games as a member of the Canadiens in 1950–51. He later wore number 12 in his three game appearance during 1952–53. Beliveau finally took up his number 4 when he signed on with the Canadiens as a regular for the 1953–54 NHL season.

13. *Who was the last player to wear number 13 for the Toronto Maple Leafs before Mats Sundin?*

Ken Linseman is better known for his thirteen NHL seasons with Philadelphia, Edmonton and Boston. Linseman played his final two NHL games wearing number 13 as a member of the Toronto Maple Leafs in the 1991–92 season.

14. *Name the future Hall of Fame goaltender who wore number 29 for Montreal prior to Ken Dryden.*

Tony Esposito saw his first NHL action in thirteen games as a member of the Montreal Canadiens in 1968–69. Sweater number 29 was among those worn by Esposito during his brief stay with the Habs.

15. *Superstitious general manager Punch Imlach liked the number 11. Name the four individuals who had outstanding rookie seasons wearing number 11 while playing on Imlach's teams.*

While wearing number 11, both Bob Nevin and Ron Ellis were runners-up for the Calder Trophy as the NHL's outstanding rookie under Imlach. Nevin placed second behind Dave Keon in 1961 voting, while Ellis was runner-up to Roger Crozier in 1965. Ron Ellis switched to number 8, passing on his number 11 to rookie Brit Selby in the 1965–66 season. Selby then won the Calder Trophy as the NHL's outstanding rookie. General manager Imlach moved on to the Buffalo Sabres where Gilbert Perreault wore number 11 winning the Calder Trophy in the Sabres' first NHL season of 1970–71.

16. *What is the lowest sweater number that has not been retired by at least one NHL franchise?*

The number 13 is the lowest sweater number that has yet to be retired by any of the NHL's thirty franchises.

17. *Name the only NHL team to retire the sweater numbers 23 and 31.*

The New York Islanders have retired number 23 for Bob Nystrom and number 31 for goalie Billy Smith.

18. *What were the most common numbers worn by the leading scorers of the thirty NHL teams in 2001–02?*
Numbers 11 and 19 were both worn by three team leaders in scoring at the close of the 2001–02 regular season. Daniel Alfredsson of the Senators, Daymond Langkow of the Coyotes and Owen Nolan of the Sharks all wore number 11 while leading their respective teams in scoring. Number 19 was worn by Markus Naslund of the Canucks, Brad Richards of the Lightning and Joe Sakic of the Avalanche as team leaders in scoring for the season.

19. *Who wore number 19 for the Soviets during the 1972 Summit Series?*
Vladmir Shadrin participated in all eight games, wearing number 19 for the Soviets. Both Shadrin and Paul Henderson, who wore number 19 for Team Canada, finished second in their team scoring in the series. Shadrin recorded three goals and five assists for a total of eight points.

20. *Who wore number 23 for the Montreal Canadiens in the season prior to Bob Gainey's arrival? (Hint: This defenseman went on to win the Jack Adams Award as top NHL coach.)*
Bob Murdoch, wearing number 23, played his only full season on the Habs blueline in 1972–73 before being traded to the Los Angeles Kings. Murdoch played his last NHL games with the Flames in 1982 and went on to a coaching career which saw him rewarded with the Jack Adams Award as coach of the Winnipeg Jets in 1990. Gainey wore the familiar number 23 with Montreal his entire NHL career from 1973 to 1989.

Second Period— Multiple Choice

1. *How many first year players have won the Lady Byng Trophy?*
a) 0   b) 1   c) 2   d) 3
b) 1. Wayne Gretzky won the Lady Byng as a first year NHL player with the Edmonton Oilers in 1979–80. This is the only time that the Lady Byng has been won by a first year NHL player.

2. *How many of the NHL's top ten scorers from the 2000–01 season were playing for a different NHL team by the end of the 2001–02 season?*
a) 2   b) 3   c) 4   d) 5

c) 4. Jaromir Jagr led the league in scoring in 2000–01 and was dealt from Pittsburgh to Washington in July of 2001. Jason Allison who had finished tied for fourth in the scoring race was traded by the Bruins to the Los Angeles Kings early in the 2001–02 season. Pavel Bure who placed seventh in league scoring as a member of the Florida Panthers was dealt to the New York Rangers in March of 2002. Doug Weight, an Edmonton Oiler who finished eighth with his scoring, was traded to the St. Louis Blues in the off-season prior to the 2001–02 season.

3. *What is the largest number of individual trophies awarded to one player in an NHL season?*
a) 3   b) 4   c) 5   d) 6
b) 4. Both Bobby Orr and Wayne Gretzky have won four individual trophies in the same season. Orr received the James Norris Trophy as the NHL's most outstanding defenseman, the Art Ross Trophy as the NHL's leading scorer, the Hart Trophy as the NHL's most valuable player and the Conn Smythe Trophy as the most valuable player in the playoffs in the 1969–70 season. Gretzky was awarded the Lester B. Pearson Award as the players' choice as the league's outstanding player along with the Art Ross, Hart, and Conn Smythe trophies in 1984–85.

4. *How many goaltenders have made their initial appearance in net for the Toronto Maple Leafs as a former Vezina Trophy winner?*
a) 5   b) 6   c) 7   d) 8
d) 8.

Goaltender	First Vezina Trophy	First Maple Leaf Season
Georges Hainsworth	1926–27	1933–34
Terry Sawchuk	1951–52	1964–65
Jacques Plante	1955–56	1970–71
Michel "Bunny" Larocque	1976–77	1980–81
Don Edwards	1979–80	1985–86
Grant Fuhr	1987–88	1991–92
Tom Barrasso	1983–84	2001–02
Ed Belfour	1990–91	2002–03

5. *What is the highest number of NHL cities that one goalie has played in?*
a) 5   b) 6   c) 7   d) 8
c) 7. Sean Burke, Gary Smith, Rick Tabaracci and Ron Tugnutt have all played goal in seven different NHL cities to the end of the 2001–02 season.

6. *How many different sweater numbers did Frank Mahovlich wear during his NHL career?*
a) 1   b) 2   c) 3   d) 4
c) 3. While Mahovlich is identified with number 27 which he wore throughout his NHL career in Toronto, Detroit and Montreal, he did briefly wear two other sweater numbers in his career. Mahovlich's first three games of NHL action were the final three games of the 1956–57 season, when the Maple Leafs called him up from the St. Mike's Juniors. Mahovlich wore number 26 in these three games. With no number 27 available, Mahovlich also briefly sported number 10, playing his first game as a member of the Montreal Canadiens in Minnesota on January 14, 1971. It is interesting to note that Mahovlich is the last player prior to Guy Lafleur to wear sweater number 10 for the Canadiens.

Ray Bourque finally accomplished his dream of playing on a Stanley Cup winner in 2001.

7. *How many members of Canada's twenty-three man roster at the 2002 Olympics had previously been on a Stanley Cup-winning team?*
a) 9   b) 10   c) 11   d) 12

d) 12. Joe Nieuwendyk, Theo Fleury and Al MacInnis were with the 1989 Calgary Flames, Mario Lemieux with Pittsburgh in both 1991 and 1992, and Martin Brodeur and Scott Niedermayer had won Cups with the Devils in 1995 and again in 2000. Steve Yzerman and Brendan Shanahan were Detroit Cup teammates in 1997 and 1998, and Eddie Belfour and Nieuwendyk played for the 1999 champs in Dallas. Joe Sakic and Adam Foote were members of the 1996 Avalanche, with Rob Blake joining them for Colorado's second Cup win in 2001.

8. *Since 1967, how many individuals have played for two teams while finishing in the top ten in NHL scoring for that season?*
a) 7   b) 8   c) 9   d) 10

c) 9.

Season	Player	Teams	Placement
1967–68	Norm Ullman	Detroit, Toronto	7th
1975–76	Jean Ratelle	Boston, Rangers	6th
1989–90	Bernie Nicholls	Los Angeles, Rangers	6th
1990–91	John Cullen	Pittsburgh, Hartford	5th
1994–95	John LeClair	Montreal, Philadelphia	9th
1995–96	Teemu Selanne	Winnipeg, Anaheim	8th
1996–97	Brendan Shanahan	Hartford, Detroit	10th
1998–99	Theoren Fleury	Calgary, Colorado	8th
2001–02	Adam Oates	Washington, Philadelphia	8th

9. *For how many NHL seasons did Ray Bourque play before he won his first Stanley Cup?*
a) 19   b) 20   c) 21   d) 22

d) Ray Bourque was finishing his twenty-second year in the NHL, in what became his final season, when he won his first Stanley Cup as a member of the Colorado Avalanche in 2001. Only two players, Doug Mohns and Dean Prentice, have ever played that many seasons without winning a Cup.

10. *How many NHL cities have hosted the Olympic Winter Games?*
a) 1   b) 2   c) 3   d) 4

a) 1. Calgary is the only NHL city to have done this when it hosted the 1988 Olympic Winter Games.

11. *How many consecutive years did Brad Park play in the Stanley Cup playoffs without being a member of a Stanley Cup championship team?*
a) 15   b) 17   c) 19   d) 21

b) 17. Brad Park saw playoff appearances in every one of his seventeen NHL seasons, from 1968–69 through 1984–85, but was never a member of a Stanley Cup-winning team.

12. *How many goalies did both the Atlanta Thrashers and Montreal Canadiens use in the 2001–02 regular season?*
a) 4   b) 5   c) 6   d) 7

b) 5. Both the Atlanta Thrashers and the Montreal Canadiens had five goalies see NHL action in 2001–02. This was the most netminders used by an NHL team this season.

13. *How many of the NHL's present thirty franchises have never been in the playoffs?*
a) 2   b) 3   c) 4   d) 5
c) 4. Only the NHL's four newest franchises, the Nashville Predators, Atlanta Thrashers, Colombus Blue Jackets and Minnesota Wild have never seen playoff action.

14. *How many times has a team won two consecutive Stanley Cups with four game sweeps since the introduction of the best-of-seven final format in 1939?*
a) 3   b) 4   c) 5   d) 6
c) 5. Toronto Maple Leafs were the first to achieve this with consecutive sweeps of the Detroit Red Wings in both 1948 and 1949. Montreal Canadiens duplicated the feat by sweeping the St. Louis Blues in both 1968 and 1969. The Canadiens achieved consecutive sweeps again in 1976 over the Flyers and in 1977 over the Bruins. The New York Islanders swept the Vancouver Canucks in 1982 and Edmonton Oilers in 1983. The Detroit Red Wings, the final team to have done this, eliminated the Philadelphia Flyers in four games in 1997 and the Washington Capitals in 1998.

16. *How many NHL teams have been Stanley Cup finalists in three consecutive seasons?*
a) 1   b) 2   c) 3   d) 4
b) 2. The 1938, 1939 and 1940 Toronto Maple Leafs and the 1968, 1969 and 1970 St. Louis Blues.

17. *How many goalies wore a sweater number higher than number 50 in 2001–02?*
a) 1   b) 2   c) 3   d) 4
c) 3. Montreal goaltenders Jose Theodore and Oliver Michaud wore numbers 60 and 95 respectively, while Kevin Weekes wore number 80 with both the Tampa Bay Lightning and the Carolina Hurricanes in 2001–02.

18. *How many players have the Boston Bruins honored with retirement of their sweater numbers?*
a) 6   b) 7   c) 8   d) 9
c) 8. When Ray Bourque was honored with the retirement of his sweater number, 77, in the 2001–02 season, he became the eighth Bruin so honored by the franchise. The others are number 2, Eddie Shore; 3, Lionel Hitchman; 4, Bobby Orr; 5, Dit Clapper; 7, Phil Esposito; 9, Johnny Bucyk; and 15, Milt Schmidt.

15. *How many players have won the Calder, Hart and Art Ross trophies in their NHL careers?*
a) 2   b) 3   c) 4   d) 5
c) 4.

Trophy-Winning Seasons			
Player	**Calder**	**Hart**	**Art Ross**
Bernie Geoffrion	1952	1961	1955, 1961
Bobby Orr	1967	1970, 1971, 1972	1970, 1975
Brian Trottier	1976	1979	1979
Mario Lemieux	1985	1988, 1993, 1996	1988, 1989, 1992, 1993, 1996, 1997

19. *How many consecutive times has an NHL player won the same trophy?*

a) 5   b) 6   c) 7   d) 8

d) 8. Only two individuals have ever won the same trophy in eight consecutive seasons. Bobby Orr won eight straight Norris Trophies as the NHL's outstanding defenseman from 1967–68 through 1974–75. Wayne Gretzky won eight consecutive Hart Trophies from 1979–80 to 1986–87.

20. *How many players scored forty or more goals in the 2001–02 NHL regular season?*

a) 5   b) 6   c) 7   d) 8

a) 5. The following players achieved this milestone in 2001–02.

Player	Goals
Jarome Iginla, Calgary	52
Mats Sundin, Toronto	41
Glen Murray, Boston	41
Bill Guerin, Boston	41
Markus Naslund, Vancouver	40

Third Period— Significant Digits

1. *Has the same sweater number ever been worn by a player on each one of the NHL teams in a given season, who all then went on to become members of the Hall of Fame?*
In both 1958–59 and 1959–60, the number 1 was worn by future members of the Hall of Fame. Future Hall of Famers Johnny Bower of Toronto, Glenn Hall of Chicago, Harry Lumley of Boston, Jacques Plante of Montreal, Terry Sawchuk of Detroit and Lorne "Gump" Worsley of New York tended the nets for the Original Six during these two seasons, all sporting the number 1.

2. *Name the only player to win the Art Ross Trophy in three different seasons while wearing a different number in each of those seasons.*
Bobby Hull won the Art Ross Trophy while wearing number 16 in 1959–60, number 7 in 1961–62 and number 9 in 1965–66.

3. *What three numbers have been retired to honor the French Connection?*
The Buffalo Sabres have retired the numbers 7, 11 and 14 to recognize the contributions of Rick Martin, Gilbert Perreault and Rene Robert. These three composed an outstanding forward line known as the French Connection, which starred for the Sabres in the 1970s.

4. *Name the four players who wore number 4 during the 1966–67 season and went on to become members of the Hockey Hall of Fame.*
Jean Beliveau of the Montreal Canadiens, Red Kelly in his final season with the Maple Leafs, Leo Boivin playing in his only full season as a member of the Detroit Red Wings and rookie Bobby Orr of the Boston Bruins all wore number 4 and became Hall of Fame members.

5. *Ted Lindsay was identified with number 7 over his Hall of Fame career with Detroit and Chicago. Lindsay returned after a four year absence from the game to play a single season in 1964–65. Why didn't he wear number 7 and what number did he wear during that season?*

Norm Ullman was a well-established player wearing number 7 for Detroit in 1964–65, when Lindsay returned. Lindsay wore number 15 in 1964–65, his final NHL season.

6. *Beside Bill Masterton, name the only other player to have a sweater number retired while having only played in a single NHL season.*

Michel Briere was an outstanding rookie with the Pittsburgh Penguins in the 1969–70 season and recorded an impressive eight points in ten playoff games to close his only season. Briere was in a car accident in May of 1970 and never regained consciousness, passing away in May of 1971. The Pittsburgh Penguins retired number 21 in honor of this outstanding rookie.

8. *Aside from Frank Mahovlich, who wore number 27, name the players on the 1960–61 NHL All-Star Team, who sported consecutive numbers from 1 to 5.*

1960–61 NHL All-Star Team		
Sweater No.	Player	Position
1	Johnny Bower, Toronto	Goal
2	Doug Harvey, Montreal	Defense
3	Marcel Pronovost, Detroit	Defense
4	Jean Beliveau, Montreal	Center
5	Bernie Geoffrion, Montreal	Right Wing
27	Frank Mahovlich, Toronto	Left Wing

9. *I wore an appropriate sweater number of 0 in my final All-Star game appearance.*

"Mr. Zero" Frank Brimsek wore a 0 for the Second Annual All-Star Game in Chicago on November 3, 1948. Brimsek split the goaltending with Bill Durnan, allowing a single goal in thirty minutes as the All-Stars defeated the Toronto Maple Leafs 3-1.

7. *When were the last ten times that the winner of an individual NHL trophy wore number 10?*

Player	Year(s)	Trophy
Ron Francis	2002	King Clancy and Lady Byng Trophies
Pavel Bure	2001, 2000	Maurice Richard Trophy
Ron Francis	1998, 1995	Lady Byng Trophy
Gary Roberts	1996	Bill Masterton Trophy
Pavel Bure	1992	Calder Trophy
Craig Ramsay	1985	Frank J. Selke Trophy
Dale Hawerchuk	1982	Calder Trophy

Bobby Hull, wearing his familiar number nine, is checked by Jacques Laperriere while Guy Lapointe and Ken Dryden focus on the play during game six of the 1971 Stanley Cup finals. All four players would later be elected to the Hockey Hall of Fame.

10. *The number 9 is identified with Gordie Howe, Bobby Hull and Rocket Richard. However, none of these three superstars began their NHL career with that sweater number. What numbers did Howe, Hull and Richard wear in their rookie seasons?*

As rookies, the famous number 9 identified with Howe, Hull and Richard was not initially worn as their sweater number. Richard began his career wearing number 15, Howe donned 17 and Hull was number 16 in their first NHL action.

13. *What sweater number did both Glenn Hall and Roger Crozier wear in the season of their first NHL appearances?*

Both Hall and Crozier donned number 22 when they replaced an injured Terry Sawchuk, Hall in 1952–53 and Crozier in 1963–64.

14. *Who is the last player to win the Art Ross Trophy wearing sweater number 12 prior to Jarome Iginla?*

Dickie Moore wore number 12 for the Montreal Canadiens, winning two consecutive Art Ross trophies in 1957–58 and 1958–59.

11. *What sweater number is currently popular among first round picks from the 1993 NHL entry draft?*

Sweater number 44 was worn by Jason Arnott, Todd Bertuzzi, Anders Eriksson, Rob Niedermayer and Chris Pronger at some point during the 2001–02 NHL season. All of these players were selected in the first round of the 1993 entry draft.

1993 Entry Draft Selection	Player	Selected By	Sweater Number 44 in 2001–02
2	Chris Pronger	Hartford Whalers	St. Louis Blues
5	Rob Niedermayer	Florida Panthers	Calgary Flames
7	Jason Arnott	Edmonton Oilers	Dallas Stars
22	Anders Eriksson	Detroit Red Wings	Toronto Maple Leafs
23	Todd Bertuzzi	New York Islanders	Vancouver Canucks

12. *Name the three former Toronto Maple Leafs who wore consecutive sweater numbers as members of the 2001–02 Montreal Canadiens.*

Doug Gilmour, Yanic Perreault and Sergei Berezin all previously played for the Toronto Maple Leafs. In 2001–02, as Montreal Canadiens, they all wore consecutive sweater numbers: Gilmour wore number 93, Perreault donned number 94 and Berezin's sweater number was 95.

15. *I am the first goalie to be selected to the NHL's year-end First All-Star Team while not wearing the number 1 for that season.*

Tony Esposito was selected to the First All-Star Team in 1969–70 while wearing the number 35.

16. *I had the highest sweater number of any member on Team Canada '72.*

Brian Glennie was assigned number 38 as a member of Team Canada '72. He did not play in any of the eight games against the Soviets in the 1972 Summit Series.

17. *Who wore number 22 for the NHL All-Stars in the 1979 Challenge Cup?*

Montreal forward Steve Shutt wore number 22. Mike Bossy, the other team member who wore number 22 as a member of the Islanders, sported number 25 in this three game series against the Soviet national team.

18. *What number did Bobby Hull wear in his final NHL game?*

Bobby Hull wore number 16 for the Hartford Whalers in his final NHL appearance. Teammate Gordie Howe was wearing what had become Hull's trademark number 9.

19. *When was the last time a goalie has worn sweater number 1 during a Vezina Trophy-winning season?*

Pete Peeters of the Boston Bruins won the Vezina Trophy in 1982–83 while wearing sweater number 1.

20. *Why does Ed Belfour wear sweater number 20?*

Belfour wears number 20 to honor Soviet goaltending great Vladmir Tretiak, who served as Belfour's goaltending coach with the Chicago Blackhawks.

Hockey Over Time

The game of hockey, this Canadian obsession, has a long and fascinating past. Over the years, from the earliest hockey to the sophisticated structure of today's game, it has developed into an exciting spectacle to watch or play. How well do you know how hockey has come to be the game it is today?

First Period— Chronologies

1. List the following Montreal teams in order of their first Stanley Cup championship, starting with the earliest winner.
Amateur Athletic Association (AAA), Canadiens, Maroons, Shamrocks, Victorias, Wanderers

First Stanley Cup Championship	
Team	**Year**
AAA	1893
Victorias	1895
Shamrocks	1899
Wanderers	1906
Canadiens	1916
Maroons	1926

2. Place the following rule changes in the order that they were introduced to the NHA/NHL.
- *Goalies permitted to drop to the ice to make a save.*
- *Games have three twenty-minute periods rather than thirty-minute halves.*
- *Rover position is eliminated, resulting in a six-man game.*
- *Referees drop the puck rather than placing it on the ice.*

1910–11—Games have three twenty-minute periods rather than thirty-minute halves.
1911–12—Rover position is eliminated, resulting in a six-man game.
1913–14—Referees drop the puck rather than placing it on the ice.
1917–18—Goalies permitted to drop to the ice to make a save.

3. List each of these events in the order that they took place.
• An NHL team wins the Stanley Cup.
• A Stanley Cup final game is held on artificial ice.
• The Stanley Cup finals are canceled.
• An American-based team wins the Stanley Cup.
• A West Coast team wins the Stanley Cup.
• An American-based team plays in the Stanley Cup finals.

1914—A Stanley Cup final game is held on artificial ice in Toronto.
1915—Vancouver Millionaires are the first West Coast-based team to win the Stanley Cup.
1916—Portland Rosebuds were the first American-based team to play in the Stanley Cup finals. They were defeated by the Montreal Canadiens.
1917—Seattle Metropolitans became the first American-based team to win the Stanley Cup.
1918—The Toronto Arenas were the first NHL team to win the Stanley Cup.
1919—The Stanley Cup finals between Seattle and Montreal Canadiens were canceled due to an influenza epidemic.

4. Place the following teams in the order of their first Stanley Cup victory: Boston Bruins, Detroit Red Wings, Chicago Black Hawks, New York Rangers

New York Rangers	1928
Boston Bruins	1929
Chicago Black Hawks	1934
Detroit Red Wings	1936

5. List the order in which the six original teams were given their familiar nicknames.

Canadiens, Bruins, Rangers, Black Hawks, Maple Leafs, Red Wings. The Canadiens have carried their name from the beginning of the franchise, playing in the 1909–1910 National Hockey Association, which became the NHL in 1917–18. Boston has been known as the Bruins since entering the league in 1924–25. New York, Chicago and Detroit were all expansion franchises for the 1926–27 season. The Rangers were formally granted a franchise in May of 1926, while Chicago and Detroit were admitted in September of the same year. Chicago and New York have maintained their nicknames since their inaugural season, with Chicago modifying its name from Black Hawks to Blackhawks in 1986. Detroit entered the league in 1926–27 as the Cougars. During the same season, Conn Smythe took charge of the Toronto St. Pats franchise and renamed the team the Maple Leafs in February of 1927. Detroit's franchise name was changed from the Cougars to the Falcons in 1930, and finally to the present name of Red Wings for the 1932–33 season.

New York
Americans' coach
Red Dutton con-
fers with Eddie
Shore. Shore
played his final
thirteen NHL
games with the
Americans fran-
chise.

6. *List the order in which each of the following superstars of the 1930s played in their last NHL season.*
King Clancy, Charlie Conacher, Aurel Joliat, Eddie Shore, Babe Siebert

Player	Last NHL Season	Team
King Clancy	1936–37	Toronto Maple Leafs
Aurel Joliat	1937–38	Montreal Canadiens
Babe Siebert	1938–39	Montreal Canadiens
Eddie Shore	1939–40	New York Americans
Charlie Conacher	1940–41	New York Americans

7. *List the following goalies in order of their first NHL game.*
Johnny Bower, Glenn Hall, Jacques Plante, Terry Sawchuk, Lorne "Gump" Worsley

Goalie	Date	Result
Terry Sawchuk, Detroit	January 8, 1950	Boston 4 at Detroit 3
Lorne Worsley, New York	October 9, 1952	New York 3 at Detroit 5
Jacques Plante, Montreal	November 1, 1952	New York 1 at Montreal 4
Glenn Hall, Detroit	December 27, 1952	Detroit 2 at Montreal 2
Johnny Bower, New York	October 8, 1953	New York 1 at Detroit 4

All five goalies played a complete game in their NHL debuts.

8. *When were the following NHL trophies first awarded, starting with the earliest?*
Calder Trophy, Conn Smythe Trophy, James Norris Trophy, Art Ross Trophy, Vezina Trophy

	First Trophy Winners	
Season	Trophy	Winner
1926–27	Vezina Trophy	George Hainsworth, Montreal Canadiens
1936–37	Calder Trophy	Syl Apps, Toronto Maple Leafs
1947–48	Art Ross Trophy	Elmer Lach, Montreal Canadiens
1953–54	James Norris Trophy	Red Kelly, Detroit Red Wings
1964–65	Conn Smythe Trophy	Jean Beliveau, Montreal Canadiens

9. *List the following players in order of their initial selection to the NHL First All-Star Team.*
Andy Bathgate, Bobby Hull, Frank Mahovlich, Stan Mikita, Henri Richard

Player	Team	Position	Initial Selection	Career Selections
Henri Richard	Montreal	Center	1957–58	1
Andy Bathgate	New York	Right Wing	1958–59	2
Bobby Hull	Chicago	Left Wing	1959–60	10
Frank Mahovlich	Toronto	Left Wing	1960–61	3
Stan Mikita	Chicago	Center	1961–62	6

NHL First All-Star Team Selections

10. *Place the following four individuals in the order of their Stanley Cup coaching victories with the Montreal Canadiens between 1968 and 1973.*
Hector "Toe" Blake, Scotty Bowman, Al MacNeil, Claude Ruel
Toe Blake, Claude Ruel, Al MacNeil, Scotty Bowman. Toe Blake coached the Montreal Canadiens to eight Stanley Cup victories, from his first in 1955–56 to his last in 1967–68, after which he retired. Claude Ruel took over from Blake and the Canadiens repeated as Stanley Cup champions in Ruel's rookie coaching season of 1968–69. Al MacNeil assumed head coaching responsibilities from Ruel during the 1970–71 season and was behind the bench at season's end when the Canadiens captured the Cup again. Scotty Bowman was named the Canadiens' head coach beginning with the 1971–72 season. His first Stanley Cup championship followed in 1972–73. Bowman remained with the Canadiens through the end of the 1978–79 season, with the Canadiens capturing four more Cups during his tenure as their head coach.

11. *List the order in which each of the following expansion teams won their first Stanley Cup.*
Calgary Flames, Colorado Avalanche, Dallas Stars, Edmonton Oilers, New Jersey Devils, New York Islanders, Philadelphia Flyers, Pittsburgh Penguins

Team	First Year in NHL	First Stanley Cup
Philadelphia Flyers	1967–68	1973–74
New York Islanders	1972–73	1979–80
Edmonton Oilers	1979–80	1983–84
Atlanta/Calgary Flames	1972–73	1988–89
Pittsburgh Penguins	1967–68	1990–91
Kansas City Scouts/Colorado Rockies/New Jersey Devils	1974–75	1994–95
Quebec Nordiques/Colorado Avalanche	1979–80	1995–96
Minnesota/Dallas Stars	1967–68	1998–99

12. *Place the following players in the order in which they reached their first fifty-goal season in the NHL.*
Glenn Anderson, Mike Gartner, Rick Kehoe, Lanny McDonald, Charlie Simmer, Rick Vaive

Player	Team	First Fifty-Goal Season	Career Fifty-Goal Seasons
Charlie Simmer	Los Angeles	1979–80—56 goals	2
Rick Kehoe	Pittsburgh	1980–81—55 goals	1
Rick Vaive	Toronto	1981–82—54 goals	3
Lanny McDonald	Calgary	1982–83—66 goals	1
Glenn Anderson	Edmonton	1983–84—54 goals	2
Mike Gartner	Washington	1984–85—50 goals	1

13. *List these players in the order in which they made their single appearance representing Canada at the World Hockey Championships in Europe.*
Paul Coffey, Wayne Gretzky, Guy Lafleur, Mario Lemieux, Mark Messier

Player	Year	Location
Guy Lafleur	1981	Stockholm, Sweden
Wayne Gretzky	1982	Helsinki, Finland
Mario Lemieux	1985	Prague, Czechoslovakia
Mark Messier	1989	Stockholm, Sweden
Paul Coffey	1990	Bern, Switzerland

14. *List the following players in the order in which they were number one picks in the NHL entry draft.*
Eric Lindros, Mike Modano, Owen Nolan, Mats Sundin, Pierre Turgeon

First Pick Overall	Player	Selected by
1987	Pierre Turgeon	Buffalo Sabres
1988	Mike Modano	Minnesota North Stars
1989	Mats Sundin	Quebec Nordiques
1990	Owen Nolan	Quebec Nordiques
1991	Eric Lindros	Quebec Nordiques

15. *List the Original Six arenas in the order in which they last saw regular season or playoff NHL action, starting with the earliest.*

Original Six Arena	Date of Last NHL Game	Score
Madison Square Garden	February 11, 1968	New York 3, Detroit 3
Detroit Olympia	December 15, 1979	Detroit 4, Quebec 4
Chicago Stadium	April 28, 1994	Toronto 1, Chicago 0
Boston Garden	May 14, 1995	New Jersey 3, Boston 2
Montreal Forum	March 11, 1996	Montreal 4, Dallas 1
Maple Leaf Gardens	February 13, 1999	Chicago 6, Toronto 2

16. *List the five countries in the order in which they were gold medal winners in the men's World Championships from 1992 to 1996.*
Canada, Czech Republic, Finland, Russia, Sweden

Country	Year	Location
Sweden	1992	Prague, Czechoslovakia
Russia	1993	Munich, Germany
Canada	1994	Bolzano, Italy
Finland	1995	Stockholm, Sweden
Czech Republic	1996	Vienna, Austria

17. *List these expansion teams in the order of their first playoff appearance.*
San Jose Sharks, Ottawa Senators, Tampa Bay Lightning, Mighty Ducks of Anaheim, Florida Panthers

Team	First Playoff Game	Score
San Jose	April 18, 1994	San Jose 5 at Detroit 4
Tampa Bay	April 16, 1996	Tampa Bay 3 at Philadelphia 7
Florida	April 17, 1996	Boston 3 at Florida 6
Anaheim	April 16, 1997	Phoenix 2 at Anaheim 4
Ottawa	April 17, 1997	Ottawa 1 at Buffalo 3

18. *List the following players in the order that they were awarded the Calder Trophy as the NHL's rookie of the year.*
Daniel Alfredsson, Bryan Berard, Chris Drury, Scott Gomez, Sergei Samsonov

Year	Calder Trophy Winners
1996	Daniel Alfredsson, Ottawa Senators
1997	Bryan Berard, New York Islanders
1998	Sergei Samsonov, Boston Bruins
1999	Chris Drury, Colorado Avalanche
2000	Scott Gomez, New Jersey Devils

19. *List the following players by age at the end of the 2001–02 regular season.*
Chris Chelios, Ron Francis, Igor Larionov, Mark Messier, Scott Stevens

Player	Birth Date	Age
Igor Larionov	December 3, 1960	41
Mark Messier	January 18, 1961	41
Chris Chelios	January 25, 1962	40
Ron Francis	March 1, 1963	39
Scott Stevens	April 1, 1964	38

20. *List the following players in the order that they were selected MVP of the All-Star games from 1996 to 2002.*
Ray Bourque, Pavel Bure, Eric Daze, Wayne Gretzky, Bill Guerin, Mark Recchi, Teemu Selanne

MVP Player	Year	All-Star Game Location
Ray Bourque	1996	Fleet Center, Boston
Mark Recchi	1997	San Jose Arena
Teemu Selanne	1998	General Motors Place, Vancouver
Wayne Gretzky	1999	Ice Palace, Tampa Bay
Pavel Bure	2000	Air Canada Centre, Toronto
Bill Guerin	2001	Pepsi Center, Denver
Eric Daze	2002	STAPLES Center, Los Angeles

Second Period—
Hockey Matches

1. *Match these early Hall of Famers with the correct name.*

"Moose" Johnson	*Edouard*
"Duke" Keats	*Ernie*
"Newsy" Lalonde	*Fred*
"Cyclone" Taylor	*Gordon*
"Rat" Westwick	*Harry*

Ernie "Moose" Johnson
Gordon "Duke" Keats
Edouard "Newsy" Lalonde
Fred "Cyclone" Taylor
Harry "Rat" Westwick

2. *Match these early Hall of Fame goaltenders with the number of seasons they played on a Stanley Cup winner.*

Clint Benedict

  Hugh Lehman

  Percy LeSueur

  Georges Vezina

1

2

3

4

Goalie	Cup Winners	Teams
Clint Benedict	4	Ottawa Senators 1920, 1921, 1923, Montreal Maroons 1926
Percy LeSueur	3	Ottawa Senators 1909, 1910, 1911
Georges Vezina	2	Montreal Canadiens 1916, 1924
Hugh Lehman	1	Vancouver Millionaires 1915

3. *Match these players with the season of their single appearance on the NHL's First All-Star Team.*

Sid Smith

Kenny Mosdell

Gus Mortson

Fleming MacKell

Roy Conacher

1948–49

1949–50

1952–53

1953–54

1954–55

Only Appearance on NHL First All-Star Team		
Roy Conacher	Chicago, Left Wing	1948–49
Gus Mortson	Toronto, Defense	1949–50
Fleming MacKell	Boston, Center	1952–53
Kenny Mosdell	Montreal, Center	1953–54
Sid Smith	Toronto, Left Wing	1954–55

4. *Each of these trophy-winning goalies played the majority of his NHL career with the team listed beside him. Match these goalies with the only other team with which they played.*

Gerry Cheevers (Boston)

Frank Brimsek (Boston)

Tiny Thompson (Boston)

Johnny Bower (Toronto)

Tony Esposito (Chicago)

Chicago

Detroit

Toronto

Montreal

New York

Goalie	Team
Gerry Cheevers (Boston)	Toronto, 1961–62
Frank Brimsek (Boston)	Chicago, 1949–50
Tiny Thompson (Boston)	Detroit, 1938–39, 1939–40
Johnny Bower (Toronto)	New York, 1953–54, 1954–55, 1956–57
Tony Esposito (Chicago)	Montreal, 1968–69

While Frank Brimsek starred with Boston from 1938–39 to 1948–49, he played his final season (1949–50) with the Chicago Black Hawks. Tiny Thompson was the Bruins' goalie from 1928–29 until Frank Brimsek arrived in 1938–39, at which time Thompson was traded to Detroit where he played through the end of the 1939–40 season. While Johnny Bower played with Toronto from 1958–59 on, he played the 1953–54 season with the New York Rangers and played in a total of seven other games in 1954–55 and again in 1956–57 with the Rangers. Tony Esposito played thirteen games in the 1968–69 season with the Montreal Canadiens before playing the remainder of his career (1969–70 through 1983–84) with the Chicago Black Hawks. Gerry Cheevers played two games with the Toronto Maple Leafs in 1961–62 before embarking on an NHL career with Boston in 1965–66 through 1979–80.

5. *Match the following Hall of Fame forwards with (a) the Original Six team they played on for their entire NHL playing career, and (b) the number of career goals they scored in NHL regular season play.*

Syl Apps	*Boston*	*148*
Bill Cook	*Chicago*	*201*
Aubrey "Dit" Clapper	*Detroit*	*228*
Aurel Joliat	*Montreal*	*229*
Herbie Lewis	*New York*	*258*
Bill Mosienko	*Toronto*	*270*

Player	*Team*	*Career Goals*
Aurel Joliat	Montreal	270
Bill Mosienko	Chicago	258
Bill Cook	New York	229
Dit Clapper	Boston	228
Syl Apps	Toronto	201
Herbie Lewis	Detroit	148

Red Wing Gordie
Howe and Leo
Boivin of the
Bruins battle for
the puck in
November of
1964.

6. *Gordie Howe won the Hart Trophy as league MVP for six of the twelve seasons between 1951–52 and 1962–63. The remaining six league MVPs during these years were all first time recipients of the Hart. Match the following players with their first Hart Trophy season.*

Andy Bathgate	*1953–54*
Jean Beliveau	*1954–55*
Bernie Geoffrion	*1955–56*
Ted Kennedy	*1958–59*
Jacques Plante	*1960–61*
Al Rollins	*1961–62*

Hart Trophy Winner	*Seasons*
Al Rollins, Chicago	1953–54
Ted Kennedy, Toronto	1954–55
Jean Beliveau, Montreal	1955–56
Andy Bathgate, New York	1958–59
Bernie Geoffrion, Montreal	1960–61
Jacques Plante, Montreal	1961–62

7. *Match these NHL players turned coaches with the team that they skated with in their first NHL game.*

Coach	*Team*
Al Arbour	*Boston*
Glen Sather	*New York*
Joe Crozier	*Detroit*
Fred Shero	*Chicago*
Emile Francis	*Montreal*
Tom Johnson	*Toronto*

Coach	Team	Season of First NHL Game
Emile Francis	Chicago	1946–47
Tom Johnson	Montreal	1947–48
Fred Shero	New York	1947–48
Al Arbour	Detroit	1953–54
Joe Crozier	Toronto	1959–60
Glen Sather	Boston	1966–67

8. *Match the teams with their correct point total for the 1966–67 NHL season.*

Boston   94
Chicago   77
Detroit   75
Montreal   72
New York   58
Toronto   44

National Hockey League 1966–67

Team	W	L	T	Points
Chicago	41	17	12	94
Montreal	32	25	13	77
Toronto	32	27	11	75
New York	30	28	12	72
Detroit	27	39	4	58
Boston	17	43	10	44

9. *Match the six expansion NHL franchises for the 1967–68 season with their first head coach.*

Los Angeles Kings   Keith Allen
Minnesota North Stars   Wren Blair
California/Oakland Seals   Leonard "Red" Kelly
Philadelphia Flyers   Bert Olmstead
Pittsburgh Penguins   Lynn Patrick
St. Louis Blues   George "Red" Sullivan

Team	Coach
Los Angeles Kings	Leonard "Red" Kelly
Minnesota North Stars	Wren Blair
California/Oakland Seals	Bert Olmstead
Philadelphia Flyers	Keith Allen
Pittsburgh Penguins	George "Red" Sullivan
St. Louis Blues	Lynn Patrick

10. *Match the Canadian and Soviet players with the numbers they wore during the 1972 Summit Series.*

Red Berenson and Alexander Yakushev	*5*
Vladimir Lutchenko and Pat Stapleton	*17*
Brad Park and Alexander Ragulin	*2*
Valery Kharlamov and Bill White	*15*
Gary Bergman and Alexander Gusev	*3*

Players	Sweater Number
Red Berenson and Alexander Yakushev	15
Vladimir Lutchenko and Pat Stapleton	3
Brad Park and Alexander Ragulin	5
Valery Kharlamov and Bill White	17
Gary Bergman and Alexander Gusev	2

11. *Match the following players with their WHA teams during the league's final season in 1978–79.*

Richard Brodeur	*Birmingham Bulls*
Bill "Cowboy" Flett	*Cincinnati Stingers*
John Garrett	*Edmonton Oilers*
Michel Goulet	*New England Whalers*
Mike Luit	*Quebec Nordiques*
Kent Nilsson	*Winnipeg Jets*

Player	WHA Yeam
Richard Brodeur	Quebec Nordiques
Bill "Cowboy" Flett	Edmonton Oilers
John Garrett	New England Whalers
Michel Goulet	Birmingham Bulls
Mike Luit	Cincinnati Stingers
Kent Nilsson	Winnipeg Jets

12. *Match the following NHL career milestone goals by Wayne Gretzky with the correct opposing goalie.*

1st	Tom Barrasso
50th	Gary Edwards
400th	Wade Flaherty
600th	Glen Hanlon
802nd	Kirk McLean
894th	Greg Stefan

Career Goal Number	Date	Opposing Goalie
1	October 14, 1979	Glen Hanlon, Vancouver
50	April 2, 1980	Gary Edwards, Minnesota
400	January 13, 1985	Tom Barrasso, Buffalo
600	November 23, 1988	Greg Stefan, Detroit
802	March 23, 1994	Kirk McLean, Vancouver
894	March 29, 1999	Wade Flaherty, New York Islanders

13. *Match the teams on the left with the year when each team was the Stanley Cup finalist.*

New York Islanders	1982
Edmonton Oilers	1981
Vancouver Canucks	1985
Minnesota North Stars	1986
Philadelphia Flyers	1984
Calgary Flames	1983

Finalist	Year	Stanley Cup Winner	Series
Minnesota North Stars	1981	New York Islanders	4–1
Vancouver Canucks	1982	New York Islanders	4–0
Edmonton Oilers	1983	New York Islanders	4–0
New York Islanders	1984	Edmonton Oilers	4–1
Philadelphia Flyers	1985	Edmonton Oilers	4–1
Calgary Flames	1986	Montreal Canadiens	4–1

14. *Match the following players with the number of Stanley Cups they won with the Edmonton Oilers.*

Charlie Huddy	*1*
Dave Hunter	*2*
Kevin McClelland	*3*
Ken Linseman	*4*
Dave Semenko	*5*

Player	Stanley Cups with Edmonton Oilers
Charlie Huddy	5—1984, 1985, 1987, 1988, 1990
Kevin McClelland	4—1984, 1985, 1987, 1988
Dave Hunter	3—1984, 1985, 1987
Dave Semenko	2—1984, 1985
Ken Linseman	1—1984

15. *Match each of the following teams with the year of their last appearance in a Stanley Cup final series.*

Calgary Flames	*1984*
Chicago Blackhawks	*1989*
Los Angeles Kings	*1992*
New York Islanders	*1993*
Vancouver Canucks	*1994*

Team	Last Cup Final	Result
New York Islanders	1984	Lost 4–1 to Edmonton
Calgary Flames	1989	Won 4–0 over Montreal
Chicago Blackhawks	1992	Lost 4–2 to Pittsburgh
Los Angeles Kings	1993	Lost 4–1 to Montreal
Vancouver Canucks	1994	Lost 4–3 to New York Rangers

16. *Match the following goalies with the team that they played for in their first NHL game.*

Byron Dafoe	*Chicago*
Mike Dunham	*New Jersey*
Jeff Hackett	*New York Islanders*
Dominik Hasek	*Quebec*
Guy Hebert	*St. Louis*
Ron Tugnutt	*Washington*

Goalie	Team
Byron Dafoe	Washington, 1992–93
Mike Dunham	New Jersey, 1996–97
Jeff Hackett	New York Islanders, 1988–89
Dominik Hasek	Chicago, 1990–91
Guy Hebert	St. Louis, 1991–92
Ron Tugnutt	Quebec, 1987–88

17. *Match the following American Hockey League awards with why it is presented.*

Aldege (Baz) Bastien Memorial Award	*Outstanding Defenseman*
The Calder Cup	*Outstanding Goalie*
Les Cunningham Award	*Leading Scorer—Regular Season*
Dudley (Red) Garrett Memorial Award	*AHL Playoff Champion*
Eddie Shore Award	*Regular Season MVP*
John B. Sollenberger Trophy	*Rookie of the Year*

AHL Award	Presented for:
Aldege (Baz) Bastien Memorial Award	Outstanding Goalie
The Calder Cup	AHL Playoff Champion
Les Cunningham Award	Regular Season MVP
Dudley (Red) Garrett Memorial Award	Rookie of the Year
Eddie Shore Award	Outstanding Defenseman
John B. Sollenberger Trophy	Leader Scorer—Regular Season

18. *Match the following goalies with the team that selected them in an NHL expansion draft.*

Mike Richter	*Mighty Ducks of Anaheim*
Corey Schwab	*Atlanta Thrashers*
Rick Tabaracci	*Colombus Blue Jackets*
Ron Tugnutt	*Florida Panthers*
John Vanbiesbrouck	*Minnesota Wild*
Mike Vernon	*Nashville Predators*

Goalie	Draft Year	Expansion Team
Ron Tugnutt	1993	Anaheim, claimed from Edmonton
John Vanbiesbrouck	1993	Florida, claimed from Vancouver
Mike Richter	1998	Nashville, claimed from New York Rangers
Corey Schwab	1999	Atlanta, claimed from Tampa Bay
Rick Tabaracci	2000	Columbus, claimed from Colorado
Mike Vernon	2000	Minnesota, claimed from Florida

19. *Match the following teams with their home arena.*

Calgary Flames	*MCI Center*
Columbus Blue Jackets	*Mellon Arena*
Minnesota Wild	*Nationwide Arena*
Pittsburgh Penguins	*Pengrowth Saddledome*
St. Louis Blues	*Savvis Center*
Washington Capitals	*Xcel Energy Center*

Team	Arena
Calgary Flames	Pengrowth Saddledome
Columbus Blue Jackets	Nationwide Arena
Minnesota Wild	Xcel Energy Center
Pittsburgh Penguins	Mellon Arena
St. Louis Blues	Savvis Center
Washington Capitals	MCI Center

20. *Match these players with the country of their birth.*

Bryon Dafoe	*Brazil*
Olaf Kolzig	*Ireland*
Robyn Regehr	*England*
Owen Nolan	*South Africa*

Player	Birthplace
Robyn Regehr	Recife, Brazil
Byron Dafoe	Sussex, England
Owen Nolan	Belfast, Ireland
Olaf Kolzig	Johannesburg, South Africa

Third Period—
We're Going to Overtime

1. *How many Stanley Cup playoff games have gone to a fourth overtime period?*

There have been ten Stanley Cup playoff games that have gone to a fourth overtime period in NHL history. The first was a semi-final match on March 28, 1930. Gus Rivers of the Montreal Canadiens scored at 8:52 of the fourth overtime period to give the Canadiens a 2-1 victory over the New York Rangers. The next two games to reach this length are the longest two games in playoff history. Both an April 1933 semi-final match between Toronto and Boston and a 1936 semi-final match between Detroit and the Montreal Maroons went into six overtime periods. The 1936 match was the longest ever, with Mud Bruneteau scoring at 16:30 of the sixth overtime period to give the Red Wings the victory. Six other games between 1938 and 1996 reached four extra sessions. The last game to reach this length was a conference semi-final on May 4, 2000, when Keith Primeau scored at 12:01 of the fifth overtime period to give the Philadelphia Flyers a 2-1 victory over the Pittsburgh Penguins.

2. *Who was the first NHL player to score in sudden-death overtime in the Stanley Cup finals?*

Odie Cleghorn of the Montreal Canadiens scored at 15:57 of overtime to lead his team to a 4-3 victory over the Seattle Metropolitans on March 30, 1919. This goal, which tied the series between Montreal and Seattle at 2-2-1, was the final game of the playoffs. The series was canceled due to the influenza epidemic sweeping North America and no Stanley Cup winner was declared for the 1919 season.

3. *Who scored for Canada in the only Olympic gold medal game decided in an overtime shootout?*

Both Petr Nedved and Paul Kariya scored for Canada on Sweden's Tommy Salo in the 1994 Olympic final. However, Peter Forsberg and Magnus Svensson both scored on Canada's Corey Hirsch in an initial five shot shootout round. Forsberg then scored again, while Kariya missed on the second shots of the sudden death round to give Sweden the 1994 gold medal. The teams had entered the shootout in a 2-2 tie after ten minutes of sudden death overtime.

4. *Name the only NHL team to win both the semi-finals and finals in overtime in the same season.*

The Detroit Red Wings are the only team to achieve this feat and have done so on two separate occasions. The Red Wings defeated the Toronto Maple Leafs on a goal by Leo Reise in the seventh and deciding game of the 1950 semi-finals. Detroit then went on to defeat the New York Rangers on Pete Babando's overtime goal in the seventh game of the finals of that season. The 1954 Detroit Red Wings advanced to the finals on a Ted Lindsay overtime goal in game five over the Toronto Maple Leafs. The Canadiens then won the Stanley Cup on an overtime goal by Tony Leswick to defeat the Montreal Canadiens in game seven of the Stanley Cup finals. The Red Wings are also the only team to win the Cup in overtime in game seven, which they accomplished in both of the above seasons.

5. *Name the only NHL franchise to have lost all of their overtime playoff games.*

The Oakland Seals were on the losing end in their only two overtime appearances in the Stanley Cup playoffs. The Los Angeles Kings defeated the Seals 5-4 in overtime in Oakland's first playoff game ever to open the 1969 quarter-finals. The Seals lost their final playoff game ever in a 3-2 overtime loss to the Pittsburgh Penguins in the 1970 quarter-finals.

6. *Name the only two NHL players to score Stanley Cup-winning goals in the third overtime period.*

Uwe Krupp of the Colorado Avalanche was the first player to do this. Krupp scored at 4:31 of the third overtime period to give Colorado a 1-0 victory over the Florida Panthers and win their first Stanley Cup on June 10, 1996. Brett Hull of the Dallas Stars scored the Cup-winning goal at 14:51 of the third overtime period on June 19, 1999, as the Stars defeated the Buffalo Sabres by a score of 2-1.

7. *Who scored the winning goal during the Montreal Canadiens' only overtime loss in the 1993 playoffs?*

Scott Young of the Quebec Nordiques scored at 16:49 of the first overtime period to defeat Montreal 3-2 in the opening game of the 1993 division semi-finals. Montreal later would defeat the Nordiques twice in overtime in the series on their way to a 4-2 series victory in the Canadiens last Cup-winning season to date.

8. *Who scored the last overtime goal of the Original Six era?*

Bob Pulford scored at 8:26 of the second overtime to give Toronto a 3-2 win over the visiting Montreal Canadiens in game three of the 1967 Stanley Cup finals.

9. *When was the last time an overtime NHL playoff game was allowed to stand as a tie?*

Game two of the 1951 semi-final series between Boston and Toronto was called after twenty minutes of overtime. The game was played on the evening of Saturday, March 31, and was curfewed as the game neared midnight because of a ban on Sunday sporting events in Toronto.

10. *Who scored the last playoff overtime goal for the Montreal Maroons?*

On April 4, 1935, Dave Trottier scored at 5:28 of the first overtime period in the opening game of the Stanley Cup finals to give the Maroons a 3-2 victory en route to a three game sweep of the Toronto Maple Leafs.

11. *On which goalie did Darryl Sittler score his Canada Cup-winning goal?*

Darryl Sittler scored on Vladimir Dzurilla of the Czech National Team at 11:33 of overtime on September 15, 1976. Sittler's goal gave Canada a 5-4 win and a two game sweep in the finals of the first ever Canada Cup Tournament.

12. *When did NHL teams first receive a point in spite of an overtime loss?*

There were two major changes in regular season overtime for the 1999–2000 season. Along with the introduction of four-on-four play during overtime, both teams received a point for the tie at the end of regulation play, with an additional point being awarded for an overtime win. The Edmonton Oilers were the first team to benefit from this change as they were awarded a point despite a 3-2 overtime loss to the San Jose Sharks on October 7, 1999.

13. *Name the only NHL franchise to have an unblemished winning record in overtime in the Stanley Cup playoffs.*

The Tampa Bay Lightning have made a single series appearance in the NHL playoffs since entering the league in 1992. The Philadelphia Flyers defeated the Lightning in six games in the conference quarter-finals in 1996. However, the two victories by the Lightning were recorded in the only two overtime games of that series. Tampa Bay defeated Philadelphia 2-1 on April 18 and 5-4 on April 21 in games two and three of the series.

14. *Name the two non-Canadian-born NHL players who have scored a Stanley Cup-winning goal in overtime.*

Pete Babando scored the Cup winner for the 1950 Detroit Red Wings. Babando was born in Braeburn, Pennsylvania. German-born Uwe Krupp scored the overtime winner in the final game of the 1996 finals as a member of the Colorado Avalanche.

15. *Who scored the first overtime goal in Buffalo Sabre history?*

Rene Robert beat goalie Ken Dryden at 9:18 of the first overtime period of game five to keep the Sabres alive in the quarter-finals in a game at the Montreal Forum on April 10, 1973.

Bobby Orr's Cup-winner was the second overtime goal in the 1970 playoffs.

16. *Who scored the only overtime goal besides Bobby Orr's Cup winner in the 1970 playoffs?*

Pittsburgh's Michel Briere scored the winning goal on Oakland's Gary Smith at 8:28 of overtime on April 12, 1970. The goal gave the Penguins a 3-2 win and a four game sweep in the quarter-finals. This was the only overtime game in Briere's brief NHL career.

17. *When was the first overtime game played in the Winter Olympics?*

Eric Lindros scored in the sudden death second shootout round following a ten minute overtime period on February 18, 1992. His goal gave Canada a 4-3 quarter-final victory over Germany at the sixteenth Olympic Winter Games held in Albertville, France.

18. *Name the NHL goalie who participated in the two longest overtime games ever?*

Lorne Chabot was on the winning end in the 1-0 Toronto victory over the Boston Bruins in the 1933 semi-finals and the losing goalie when the Detroit Red Wings defeated the Montreal Maroons in the 1936 semi-finals. Both games went into six overtime periods.

19. *Have opposing NHL teams ever gone to a third overtime period in two consecutive playoff games?*

This has happened on one occasion in NHL history. The Montreal Canadiens and Detroit Red Wings opened their 1951 semi-final series with two marathon games. Maurice Richard scored the winner in both games, scoring at 1:09 of the fourth overtime period for a 3-2 Canadiens victory in game one and at 2:20 of the third overtime period for a 1-0 Montreal win in the second game of the series.

20. *Regular season overtime was reinstated beginning in 1983–84. Who scored the first NHL regular season overtime goal since 1942?*

Bob Bourne scored to give his New York Islanders an 8-7 victory over the Washington Capitals on Saturday, October 8, 1983. The five minute sudden death overtime period which follows a regular season tie was introduced to the league for the 1983–84 season. It was the first time since November of 1942 that overtime had been played in the NHL regular season.

Will These Records Be Unbroken?

In the game of hockey, records of achievement are continually being broken by those who are faster, stronger and more skilled. It seems impossible to imagine, however, that some of these records will ever be surpassed by a more outstanding accomplishment. Whether these records will ever be broken is something only the coming years will determine. How are you at remembering the records of hockey's heroes?

First Period— Who Am I?

1. *I hold the NHL record for career shutouts.*
Terry Sawchuk recorded 115 career shutouts, 103 in the regular season and 12 more in the playoffs in his NHL career, from 1949–50 through to 1969–70. Patrick Roy is the active player who is closest to this record. At the end of the 2001–02 season, Roy has recorded sixty-one regular season shutouts, and twenty-two more in the playoffs.

2. *I recorded an amazing 550 shots on goal in a single season.*
Phil Esposito of Boston recorded this amazing statistic in 1970–71. In that year, he also recorded seventy-six goals in seventy-eight games. The second most shots on goal in a season is 429, a record held by Paul Kariya. He accomplished this feat with Anaheim in the 1998–99 season, while playing eighty-two games.

3. My single season goaltending records will never be duplicated.

George Hainsworth recorded an incredible twenty-two shutouts in forty-four games, tending goal for the Montreal Canadiens for the 1928–29 season. In this year, Hainsworth also had an amazing 0.92 goals-against average. The rules were changed to make the game more offensive starting in the 1929–30 season. One of the biggest changes that was made was the addition of the forward pass in the offensive zone. With a much more offensive game now in place, it would be impossible to record numbers like those of George Hainsworth's in the 1928–29 season.

4. I was among the NHL's top five point leaders for twenty consecutive seasons.

Gordie Howe of the Detroit Red Wings placed in the top five in league scoring every season from 1949–50 to 1968–69. Wayne Gretzky only accomplished this in sixteen of his twenty NHL seasons; missing in 1992–93, 1994–95, 1995–96 and 1998–99. This is one area where Howe's record withstood the incredible challenge of Gretzky's talent.

5. I am the only individual to lose in the NHL finals and be on a Stanley Cup winner in the same year.

Ottawa defenseman Eddie Gerard faced the Toronto St. Patricks in the 1922 NHL finals. The St. Pats defeated the Senators in a two game total goals series and advanced to the Stanley Cup finals against the Vancouver Millionaires of the Pacific Coast Hockey Association. When the St.

Pats ran into injury problems, they requested and obtained permission from Vancouver to use Gerard in game four of the series, which Vancouver led 2-1. Gerard played a solid game on defense, as the St. Pats defeated the Millionaires 6-0 to even the series. Vancouver reversed their decision on Gerard for the fifth and final match of the Stanley Cup championship. Toronto, without Gerard in their lineup, still easily defeated the Millionaires 5-1 to capture the Cup.

6. I made my first appearance in the NHL at the age of sixteen.

Born on December 9, 1925, Armand "Bep" Guidolin was only sixteen when he entered the NHL in the 1942–43 season. He was a month short of his seventeenth birthday when he took part in his first NHL game with the Bruins on November 12, 1942. He played in forty-two games during the 1942–43 season, when he recorded seven goals and fifteen assists for twenty-two points, as well as four assists in nine playoff games. It was due to the Second World War, when the NHL was short on players, that Bep got his chance to play despite his youth. At this time, the NHL signed up any talented player regardless of age.

7. I scored thirty or more goals in fifteen consecutive seasons.

For fifteen consecutive seasons, between 1979–80 and 1993–94, Mike Gartner scored thirty or more goals. He was unable to reach the thirty goal plateau the following season, which was limited to forty-eight games in 1995 due to a labor dispute.

8. *I served as the head coach of an NHL franchise for an incredible twenty straight seasons.*

Jack Adams served as head coach of one NHL franchise for twenty years. Adams played his last season of NHL hockey in 1926–27 with Ottawa, when he heard that the Detroit Cougars were looking for a coach. He became general manager of the club, a position he held from 1927–28 until 1961–62. Being his own boss in terms of hockey operations, Adams ended up coaching the team himself during 1927–28 and remained in that position until 1946–47.

9. *I recorded a record fourteen assists in a single season as a goaltender.*

Edmonton's goaltender Grant Fuhr recorded fourteen assists in forty-five games during 1983–84. It was an era of wide open hockey and Fuhr's ability was augmented by the magical combination of offensively powerful teammates. It is unlikely that another goaltender will ever again have this type of scoring power playing in front of them. The goaltender with the second highest number of assists was Curtis Joseph, who recorded nine when he played with the St. Louis Blues in 1991–92.

10. *I recorded ten points in a single NHL game.*

On February 7, 1976, Darryl Sittler recorded ten points in a 11-4 win over the Boston Bruins. He scored an outstanding six goals and four assists in this game. Two months later on April 22, 1976, Sittler netted another five goals in a single game, in an 8-5 playoff win over Philadelphia in game six of the quarter-finals. Numerous other players have recorded eight points in a game, including Wayne Gretzky and Mario Lemieux.

11. *I am the oldest individual to win the Calder Trophy as the NHL rookie of the year.*

Sergei Makarov, Calgary, 1990. Makarov was thirty-one years old when he first played in the NHL in 1989–90, recording eighty-six points in eighty games. Even though he was considered a rookie, he had been playing the equivalent of professional hockey in the Soviet Union for over a decade before he arrived in the NHL. The next year, the rules were changed, defining a rookie as being twenty-five or younger in the month prior to the beginning of the season.

12. *I hold the record for the greatest number of consecutive NHL games in which a point was recorded.*

Wayne Gretzky of the Edmonton Oilers recorded a point in fifty-one consecutive games during the 1983–84 season. Gretzky recorded 61 goals and 92 assists for 153 points over this streak. Mario Lemieux is the only other player to even come close to this record, when he had a forty-six game scoring steak in 1989–90. The wide open play of that time is now considered to be a bygone era. Even if another superstar of the magnitude of Gretzky or Lemieux comes along, it is still unlikely that such a consecutive streak will ever again be possible.

This Philadelphia Flyer earned five points in his first NHL game. Eddie Johnstone of the Rangers is in the background.

13. *I recorded five points in my first major league game in the NHL in 1977.*

Five points were recorded by Al Hill of Philadelphia in his first NHL game on February 14, 1977. Hill recorded two goals and three assists in a 6-4 victory over St. Louis. Joe Malone also recorded five goals in his first game in the NHL. Malone, however, wasn't a rookie since he had been a regular player in the NHA. The NHA had just become the NHL so Malone's initial game was not his first major-league experience.

14. *My goals were the game winners in all four of my team's victories in one playoff series.*

Mike Bossy recorded all four game-winning goals for the Islanders in their 4-2 series win over the Boston Bruins in the 1983 conference finals. This record may one day be tied, but never bettered since by winning all four games you win the series.

15. *I am the last player to have played for all of the NHL franchises in the league during my NHL career.*

With thirty teams now in the NHL, no player will ever duplicate Vic Lynn's feat of playing for all of the existing NHL franchises during a career. Lynn's only appearance as a member of the New York Rangers was in a single game in the 1942–43 season. He then played a total of 286 regular season games with the Detroit Red Wings, Montreal Canadiens, Toronto Maple Leafs and Boston Bruins over the next decade. Lynn was a member of three Stanley Cup-winning Maple Leaf teams in the late 1940s. He saw his final NHL action over two seasons with the Chicago Black Hawks, his last NHL season being 1953–54.

16. *I recorded a record seven goals in a single NHL game.*

Joe Malone recorded seven goals in an NHL game between his Quebec Bulldogs and the Toronto St. Patricks on January 31, 1920. The game, held at Quebec, was won by the home team 10-6. It was one of only four Quebec wins in twenty-four games that season.

17. *I was the starting goalie for a record seventy-nine games with the St. Louis Blues in the 1995–96 season.*

Grant Fuhr was the starter in net for seventy-nine of the Blues' eighty-two games in the 1995–96 season. It is hard to imagine a goaltender starting more games in an eighty-two regular game schedule.

18. *I served as general manager, coach and captain of the Detroit Cougars in their first NHL season of 1926–27.*

Art Duncan played on Detroit's defense while serving as captain, coach and GM of the expansion franchise. Duke Keats, arrived in a trade from Boston in January 1927, taking over the coaching role from Duncan for the final eleven games of the season. In May of 1927, Duncan moved on to Toronto where he played in four more seasons, before becoming Toronto's coach in 1930–31. Jack Adams took over as Detroit's coach and GM for the 1927–28 season. Adams traded Keats to Chicago in December of 1927.

19. *I recorded five goals as a defenseman in a single NHL game.*
Five goals were recorded by defenseman Ian Turnbull when the Leafs challenged Detroit on February 2, 1977. Toronto won the game by a score of 9-1 at Maple Leaf Gardens. Several other defensemen have recorded four goals in a game, including another effort by Turnbull playing for Los Angeles in 1981. Interestingly, Bobby Orr never recorded four goals in a game.

20. *I was the last NHL goalie to shut out all the opposing NHL teams at least once during one regular season.*
Ed Giacomin of the Rangers was the last NHL goalie to shut out all opposition at least once, in the 1966–67 season. He shut out Toronto on three occasions, Detroit and Chicago twice and Boston and Montreal once. Chicago's Tony Esposito, who had to face eleven or more teams in his career, had more trouble shutting out each franchise. He came close to such a record in 1969–70, when he achieved fifteen career shutouts and managed to blank nine different opposing teams. The only teams he didn't record a shutout against in 1969–70 were the New York Rangers and the Minnesota North Stars. Currently, it would be necessary to shut out twenty-nine teams to achieve such a record, unlikely to happen.

Second Period— Multiple Choice

1. *How many consecutive titles did the Soviet Union win in the Olympics and World Championships?*
a) 7   b) 8   c) 9   d) 10
d) 10. The Soviets won ten straight Olympic and World Championships from 1963 to 1972. In 1972, the Soviets retained the gold medal at the Olympics, but Czechoslovakia ended the Soviets' streak by winning the World Championships later that year. During these years, the Soviets and other European countries had an advantage as they iced their best players in world competitions. Canada was unable to ice a winning team as its best players were in the NHL. With all hockey nations now having top players with NHL commitments, such domination by one country is unlikely.

2. *Who holds the record for the most penalty minutes recorded in an NHL regular season?*
a) Dale Hunter   b) Dave Schultz
c) Tiger Williams   d) Chris Nilan
b) Dave Schultz of the Philadelphia Flyers recorded a record 472 penalty minutes in 1974–75. This is equivalent to almost eight full games. Tiger Williams led the league twice in penalty minutes, but his highest total in one season was 343 minutes with Vancouver in 1980–81. Williams is also the all-time career leader in penalty minutes with 3966. Dale Hunter is second on the all-time list with 3565, but was never the leader for one particular season. Chris Nilan led in penalty minutes twice in 1983–84 and 1984–85. The highest number of penalties he took was 358 in 1984–85 with Montreal.

The Montreal Canadiens celebrate their 1993 Stanley Cup Victory.

3. *How many teams have played an entire NHL playoff series with no home games?*

a) 1   b) 2   c) 3   d) 4

d) 4. In past years, teams would be unable to use their home arenas due to other bookings. The best known example is the circus evicting the New York Rangers every playoff spring. The first team to play no home games in a series was the Chicago Black Hawks in the 1927 quarter-finals. In the two game series against Boston, one game was played in Boston and one in New York. The following year in the quarter-finals, the Pittsburgh Pirates played both games of a two game series in New York. Later that same playoff year, 1928, the New York Rangers played all five final games against the Montreal Maroons at the Montreal Forum. The last time a team had no home games in a playoff series was during the 1950 Stanley Cup finals. The New York Rangers played five games in Detroit and used Maple Leaf Gardens in Toronto for their home rink in games two and three of the series.

4. *How many times did Bobby Orr win the Art Ross Trophy?*
a) 0   b) 1   c) 2   d) 3
c) 2. Bobby Orr first won the Art Ross Trophy as the leading scorer in the NHL in 1969–70 with 120 points, an outstanding achievement for a defenseman. He was again the recipient in 1974–75 when he recorded an incredible 135 points. No other defenseman has ever come close to winning the league scoring championship.

5. *Who holds the NHL record for the most goals scored by a first year player?*
a) Mike Bossy   b) Pavel Bure
c) Luc Robitaille   d) Teemu Selanne
d) Rookie Teemu Selanne scored seventy-six goals for the Winnipeg Jets in 1992–93. No one has been close to challenging his record. Mike Bossy is second all time with fifty-three goals for the Islanders in 1977–78.

6. *Which NHL franchise has lost the most games in a single season?*
a) New York Islanders
b) Ottawa Senators
c) San Jose Sharks
d) Washington Capitals
c) The San Jose Sharks lost seventy-one of their eighty-four games in their second season of play in 1992–93.

7. *What is the NHL record for the number of ties recorded by a team in a season?*
a) 18   b) 20   c) 22   d) 24
d) 24. The Philadelphia Flyers recorded twenty-four ties in the 1969–70 season. This will probably stand as the record since rule changes have since been introduced. In 1983–84, the five minute overtime was initiated, followed by a change to four-on-four overtime in 1999–2000, in which the loser still gains a point.

8. *How many of Montreal's sixteen playoff wins en route to the 1993 Stanley Cup were overtime decisions?*
a) 7   b) 8   c) 9   d) 10
d) 10. Ten overtime wins were recorded by the Montreal Canadiens in the single playoff year of 1993. This is very unusual since you only need to win sixteen games to be awarded the Stanley Cup.

9. *What is the largest number of new NHL franchises to have begun play in one season?*
a) 4   b) 6   c) 8   d) 10
b) Six NHL franchises were added to the National Hockey League in 1967–68. Other major expansions included the addition of four teams in 1979–80, and three franchises were added for the 1926–27 season.

10. *What is the highest number of goals scored in overtime in an NHL game?*
a) 1   b) 2   c) 3   d) 4

d) 4. At the beginning of the 1928–29 season, the NHL changed the way it decided regular season ties. Sudden death overtime was changed to a ten minute overtime period, to be played in its entirety regardless of the number of goals scored. This ten minute overtime period remained in effect until November of 1942. It was then dropped from the league to avoid delaying train schedules during the Second World War. During the fourteen-plus seasons that this rule was in effect, there were two separate games in which four overtime goals were scored. Madison Square Garden was the site of both of these games. The visiting Montreal Maroons recorded four overtime goals to defeat the New York Rangers by a score of 7-3 on March 11, 1934. The Boston Bruins netted four overtime goals to defeat the New York Americans by a score of 6-2 on November 27, 1941.

11. *Which goaltender played the most consecutive NHL games?*
a) Jacques Plante   b) Harry Lumley
c) Terry Sawchuk   d) Glenn Hall

d) Glenn Hall played in 551 consecutive NHL regular season and playoff games. His goaltending streak began at the start of the 1955–56 season as a member of the Detroit Red Wings and lasted until November 7, 1962, when as a Chicago Black Hawk he was forced out of a game due to injury. Hall achieved this amazing consecutive game streak without wearing a face mask.

12. *What is the highest number of overtime goals scored by a player in one NHL playoff year?*
a) 2   b) 3   c) 4   d) 5

b) 3. "Sudden death" Mel Hill recorded three overtime goals for the Boston Bruins in games one, two and seven of the semi-final playoff series against the New York Rangers in 1939. The only other player to score three overtime goals in the playoffs took two series to accomplish this feat, in 1951. Rocket Richard netted two overtime goals against Detroit in the first two games of the semi-finals, and scored the winner in game two of the finals against Toronto.

13. *What is the highest number of consecutive playoff games lost by an NHL franchise in the Stanley Cup finals?*
a) 10   b) 12   c) 14   d) 16

b) 12. The St. Louis Blues lost all twelve of their Stanley Cup final appearances in the three finals from 1968 to 1970. The Blues put up heroic battles against Montreal in 1968 and 1969 and Boston in 1970. They had a distinct disadvantage in being an expansion team going up against the established teams from the Original Six era. It is unlikely that the NHL will ever again arrange the playoffs in such an unbalanced manner, allowing a weaker team to make three consecutive appearances in the Stanley Cup finals.

14. *In which playoff year did two players score five goals in single playoff games?*
a) 1919   b) 1944   c) 1976   d) 1989
c) 1976. Both Darryl Sittler of the Toronto Maple Leafs and Reggie Leach of the Philadelphia Flyers each recorded five goals in single games in the 1976 Stanley Cup playoffs. There have only been five occasions in NHL history when five goals have been scored in one playoff game.

15. *How many teams have won the Stanley Cup in the minimum number of games required since the introduction of a best-of-seven playoff format in 1939?*
a) 0   b) 1   c) 2   d) 3
c) 2. Only the 1952 Detroit Red Wings and the 1960 Montreal Canadiens won the Stanley Cup in the minimum number of required games. Both the Red Wings and Canadiens required eight games as they swept both the best-of-seven semi-final and final series. In the 1926–27 season, the NHL took sole possession of the Stanley Cup. The best-of-seven playoff format for the Stanley Cup finals was introduced in 1938–39. Between these dates, four other teams also took the Cup in the minimum number of games: the 1929 Bruins, 1930 Canadiens, 1932 Maple Leafs and 1935 Maroons. Considering this would now require a sixteen game undefeated streak in the playoffs, it is highly unlikely to occur again in NHL history.

16. *Since 1927, what is the maximum number of consecutive seasons when there were no sweeps in any Stanley Cup playoff series between NHL teams?*
a) 5   b) 6   c) 7   d) 8
a) 5. There was not a single playoff series won in four consecutive games in any of the five NHL playoff seasons between 1961 and 1965. With fifteen playoff series now taking place for a Cup winner to be decided, it makes even a single season with no playoff sweeps unlikely.

17. *Which NHL franchise holds the record for most consecutive appearances in the playoffs?*
a) Boston Bruins
b) Chicago Blackhawks
c) Detroit Red Wings
d) Montreal Canadiens
a) The Boston Bruins appeared in the playoffs for twenty-nine consecutive seasons between 1968 and 1996. The Blackhawks came close to the record with twenty-eight consecutive playoff appearances between 1970 and 1997. The current leaders in this category, the St. Louis Blues, made their twenty-third consecutive playoff appearance in the 2002 Stanley Cup playoffs.

18. *How many points did Wayne Gretzky record during his NHL career?*
a) 2010   b) 2589   c) 3239   d) 3349
c) Wayne Gretzky had 3239 points in his NHL career between 1979–80 and 1998–99. He recorded 2857 points in the regular season and added another 382 in playoff competition.

19. *How many individuals have played on ten or more Stanley Cup winners?*
a) 1   b) 2   c) 3   d) 4
c) 3. Henri Richard captured eleven Stanley Cups skating with the Montreal Canadiens between 1956 and 1973. Jean Beliveau and Yvan Cournoyer both won ten Stanley Cup rings while playing with the Canadiens, a close second to Richard.

20. *Which NHL franchise recorded the longest undefeated streak ever?*
a) Edmonton Oilers
b) Montreal Canadiens
c) Philadelphia Flyers
d) Toronto Maple Leafs
c) Philadelphia Flyers. In 1979–80, Philadelphia recorded the longest undefeated streak ever, going thirty-five games without a loss. They had twenty-five wins and ten ties between October 14, 1979, when they beat Toronto 4-3 in Philadelphia, and January 6, 1980, when they were winners over Buffalo 4-2. On January 7, 1980, their streak ended when they lost 7-1 at Minnesota to the North Stars. The second closest streak is credited to Montreal, who went twenty-eight games undefeated in 1977–78.

Third Period— Expert Trivia

1. *Which NHL season saw the most players record one hundred points or more?*
1992–93. Twenty-one players reached this plateau in the 1992–93 season. Mario Lemieux was on top with 160 points. Theoren Fleury of Calgary and Ron Francis of Pittsburgh were twentieth and twenty-first with one hundred points each. Wayne Gretzky was not included in this group as he was injured much of the season. The second highest season, in 1984–85, has sixteen players reaching the one hundred point mark. Nobody recorded one hundred points in 2001–02. Jarome Iginla was the highest scorer, finishing the season with ninety-six points.

Season	Regular Season Points	Playoff Points	Total Points
1981–82	212	12	224
1982–83	196	38	234
1983–84	205	35	240
1984–85	208	47	255
1985–86	215	19	234

2. *What were the five highest scoring seasons by an individual player, including playoffs, in NHL history?*
Wayne Gretzky's five consecutive seasons from 1981–82 to 1985–86 takes this record.

3. *Which NHL franchise has won the most consecutive playoff series?*
The New York Islanders won nineteen consecutive playoffs series between 1980 and 1984.

4. *Since 1927, which NHL playoff year had the fewest number of overtime games?*

1963. Out of the sixteen required playoff games, none of them went into overtime in 1963. With the increased number of games now necessary to win the cup, we will never see another playoff season without the excitement of sudden death overtime hockey.

5. *What was the greatest scoring display by one player and team in a single game during a Stanley Cup contest?*

There were an incredible twenty-three goals scored by the Ottawa Silver Seven in a 1905 Stanley Cup playoff game versus the Dawson City Klondikers. "One-eyed" Frank McGee alone scored fourteen goals in this single game.

7. *Which NHL seasons had the highest percentage of Canadian-based franchises?*

The National Hockey League had 100% of its franchises based in Canada during the first seven seasons of operation from 1917–18 to 1923–24. The league had as many as five franchises during these years but never iced more than four teams in any one season. Teams played out of Montreal, Ottawa, Toronto, Quebec and Hamilton during some or all of these seasons. The league expanded to Boston in 1924–25, and by 1926–27 had dropped to 40% of the teams based in Canadian cities. Six of the ten franchises were now from south of the border. The highest percentage of Canadian-based franchises in recent years is 33%, from 1980–81 to 1990–91, with seven of twenty-one teams in Canada, and again in 1992–93, with eight of twenty-four teams based in Canada.

6. *Name the NHL teams that drafted the six Sutter brothers.*

They are the highest number of brothers who all played in the NHL.

Player	Team Drafted By	Draft Year
Brent	New York Islanders	1980
Brian	St. Louis Blues	1976
Darryl	Chicago Black Hawks	1978
Duane	New York Islanders	1979
Rich	Pittsburgh Penguins	1982
Ron	Philadelphia Flyers	1982

8. *Which NHL franchise never won another playoff game following their Stanley Cup-winning season?*

The Ottawa Senators won their fourth Stanley Cup of the decade in 1927. However, this once powerful franchise began experiencing financial difficulties and only qualified for the playoffs on two more occasions during their existence. They were swept by the Montreal Maroons in a two game total goal series by scores of 1-0 and 2-1 in the 1928 quarter-finals. Their final appearance in the 1930 quarter-finals resulted in a 1-1 tie with the New York Rangers, followed by a 5-2 defeat when the Rangers took the two game total series by a count of 6-3. The franchise played their final game as the Senators in 1934, with the franchise relocating to St. Louis for a single season before being disbanded. While the Calgary Flames have yet to win a playoff series following their 1989 Stanley Cup victory, it is hard to imagine an NHL franchise not recording a single playoff victory ever again following the Stanley Cup win.

Hall of Famer Larry Robinson played on six Stanley Cup winners.

9. *How old was Gordie Howe in his final NHL appearance?*

Gordie Howe was fifty-two when he took part in his final NHL playoff game. His birthday is March 31, 1928. His last game was April 11, 1980, a week and a half past his fifty-second birthday.

10. *What is maximum number of players from one team on the NHL First All-Star Team in one season?*

Five players from a single team were named to the NHL First All-Star Team in two seasons during the Original Six era. The Montreal Canadiens placed five players on the 1944–45 team, while the 1963–64 Chicago Black Hawks repeated this feat. Thirty teams make such dominance by players from a single team next to impossible.

11. *Which first year NHL team played the most overtime playoff games?*

St. Louis participated in eight overtime games in the 1968 Stanley Cup playoffs. The Blues had both an overtime win and loss in their quarter-final series win over Philadelphia. St. Louis then won three of four overtime decisions as they eliminated Minnesota in the semi-finals. Montreal defeated the Blues twice in overtime, as they took the Cup in four straight games. With four expansion teams qualifying for the playoffs, the Blues were able to advance all the way to the finals. With the current format, it is almost impossible for a new team to qualify, let alone be successful in the playoffs.

12. *Which two NHL teams faced each other for the longest playing time in a single NHL series?*

The 1939 Boston Bruins and New York Rangers played a seven game semi-final series that lasted a record of 553 minutes and 8 seconds. It was this series that introduced the best-of-seven format to the NHL playoffs. Two games of this contest went into single overtime, while two games lasted well into a third overtime period.

13. *Since 1927, what is the fewest number of shutouts recorded in an NHL playoff year?*

There was not a single shutout recorded in any of the eighteen games played in the 1959 Stanley Cup playoffs.

14. *Name the NHL player on the most Stanley Cup championship teams not yet selected as a member of the Hockey Hall of Fame.*

Claude Provost played on the Montreal Canadiens between 1955–56 and 1969–70, winning nine Stanley Cups during those years. He has yet to be elected to the Hockey Hall of Fame. He was a First Team All-Star in 1964–65. He likely would have won the Frank J. Selke trophy as the best defensive forward in the league on several occasions, if the trophy had been awarded. It is unusual that such a successful career has not been recognized by the Hockey Hall of Fame.

15. *What are the two highest point totals ever recorded by a defenseman in a single NHL season?*
Bobby Orr netted 139 points in 1970–71 but trailed the Art Toss winner, Phil Esposito, who had a total of 152 points. Paul Coffey scored 138 points in 1985–86, the second highest point total a defenseman ever has. He was third in scoring that season, behind Wayne Gretzky with 215 and Mario Lemieux with 141 points.

16. *Which NHL team holds the record for consecutive appearances in the Stanley Cup finals?*
The Montreal Canadiens reached the Stanley Cup finals for a consecutive ten seasons, from 1951 to 1960. The Canadiens won the Cup on six of these occasions.

17. *What is the fewest number of trades to take place during an NHL season?*
No trades at all took place involving NHL regulars during the 1966–67 season.

18. *How many times has a sudden death overtime goal resulted in a tie in an NHL playoff game?*
There have been two occasions when teams entered overtime losing in that particular game but being tied for the two game total goal series. In the 1930 quarter-final series between the Montreal Canadiens and the Chicago Black Hawks, the Canadiens took the first game 1-0 in Chicago. Chicago was leading 2-1 over Montreal in the second game three nights later on March 26, 1930. Based on a 2-2 tie in total goals, the game proceeded to a third overtime period before Howie

Morenz scored at 11:43 to give Montreal a 2-2 tie in the game and a 3-2 win in the total goal series. In another quarter-final series between the same two teams in 1934, Chicago defeated Montreal 3-2 at the Forum on March 22. Three nights later in Chicago, Montreal was leading 1-0 at the end of regulation time when Mush March scored at 11:05 of overtime to give Chicago a 1-1 tie in the game and a 4-3 win in the two game total goal series.

19. *How many consecutive seasons did Larry Robinson play in the NHL playoffs?*
20. Larry Robinson played in twenty consecutive Stanley Cup playoffs, from 1973 through 1992.

20. *How many minutes of hockey were played in the longest NHL overtime game?*
176 minutes and 30 seconds. Just three and a half minutes short of three complete games were played in the longest overtime game in NHL history. Mud Bruneteau scored for the Detroit Red Wings in a 1-0 win over the Montreal Maroons at 16:30 of the sixth overtime period in the opening game of the 1936 semi-finals. The game had started at 8:30 on the evening of March 24 at the Montreal Forum and ended at 2:25 the next morning. Detroit went on to defeat the Maroons and the Maple Leafs in the finals to capture their first of what is now ten Stanley Cups.